CRAFTS
for Religious
Education

TEL Publishers, Ltd.   Rockford, IL

The purchaser of this book is hereby granted permission to make copies of patterns in this book for use with his or her students.

Cover Art, Design and Illustrations: Steve Clevenger

Editor: Laurine M. Easton

This *Crafts for Religious Education* book was originally designed to be used with the **CHURCH** program of religious education for parish elementary programs. The **CHURCH** program is a complete program designed for volunteer catechists. For more information, contact BROWN Publishing - ROA Media.

Exclusively Distributed By

BROWN-ROA

A Division of Harcourt Brace & Company

ISBN 1-55588-144-0

Printed in the United States of America

TABLE OF CONTENTS

GUIDELINES FOR ADULT LEADERS IN THE USE OF CRAFTS IN RELIGIOUS EDUCATION

When planning craft projects with students, there are some important guidelines that will insure success.

1. Some months before the beginning of the educational year, brainstorm possible ways to express visually what you are teaching. List possible projects and materials you might need for the year. Make a list of materials you will need and distribute it to parents and other parishioners. Designate the time and place where these things can be donated.

2. Make the project yourself first. Keep in mind the age level of the students who will be making the project. Time the project to decide how much of the work needs to be prepared in advance in order for the students to be able to complete the project within the projected time allotment.

3. Have sufficient numbers of helpers, or aides, to assist the students in working on the project. Do not assume that students will be as informed as you are about the steps involved in the project.

4. Give attention to the physical environment to avoid any unnecessary distraction for the students. Play suitable music to support the theme of the project and to provide a peaceful and calm setting. If students arrive at a craft center, provide supervision prior to and upon entering the area.

5. When possible, it is helpful to decorate the craft area in the theme of the project to be created. This provides a visual incentive for students. A very simple way to set the theme is to display the project of the day made by you in advance of the craft session. Any other appropriate pictures or symbols can enhance the environment. A more elaborate environment might be a tree which has hung on it biblical symbols for Advent, ornaments for Christmas, cocoons for Lent and butterflies or eggs for Easter.

6. Explain the reason each particular project has been chosen. Give the practical application for each project. Try to impart a sense of pride in doing the project to the best of the student's ability while encouraging the student's creativity.

7. Use newspapers liberally to keep work area clean.

8. Prepare to work with small groups at a table with some aides at each table. Have one table set up with supplies.

9. Try to use a variety of materials and ideas throughout the year. Give the students freedom to create, options to choose from and the encouragement to try the craft in order to experience some feeling of success.

10. Be prepared to keep certain projects for drying, etc., until the students return for the projects the same day or until the next session. Projects can be put aside in the same way students are grouped. They then can be conveniently returned to the students.

COLLAGE OF SIGNS & SYMBOLS   Grades 1-4

Materials Needed:

Magazines
Poster paper
Glue or paste
Scissors
Crayons or felt-tip markers

Procedure:

1. Have the students move into small groups and make a collage of different signs they see every day. Encourage the students to use some of the signs of the Church as the focal point of their collage.
2. Cut out pictures from magazines or have the students draw their own signs or symbols to cut out and put together on one collage.
3. This project could be a one-day or a two-day project. Draw and cut the first day. Then paste and discuss the different collages the second day.

Note: As an alternative, you could have the students bring their own special-interest magazines.

FELT BOOKMARKERS   Grades 1-8

Some of the symbols of our Christian faith can be made up as bookmarkers for Bibles and other reading books. Bookmarkers can be given as gifts to others. Provide a sample bookmarker to help the students proceed with a bookmarker project of their choice. Supply samples or patterns of the symbols.

This project can be used for all grade levels, depending upon the complexity of the symbol chosen. Use simple, single-piece patterns for grades 1 and 2.

Materials Needed:

One 2" x 6" strip of stiff felt for each student
Colored felt
Cardboard patterns of symbols
Pencils
Scissors
White glue

Optional: Trim material such as gold braid, silver and gold thread, embroidery floss, ribbon, etc.

Before Class:

Prepare ample cardboard patterns for the students. Cut out felt symbols ahead of class time for the younger students. They can then arrange the symbol on their bookmarkers and glue. Add decorations with trim materials.

Procedure:

1. Choose two different colors of felt: one for the bookmarker itself and one for the symbol to be put onto the bookmarker.
2. Choose one of the symbol patterns from this book or draw your own Christian symbol.
3. Trace the pattern on a piece of felt. Cut out the symbol.
4. Glue the symbol to the bookmarker.
5. Decorate with scrap pieces of felt and/or trim material. Using scissors, cut the bottom of the bookmarker to make fringe.

 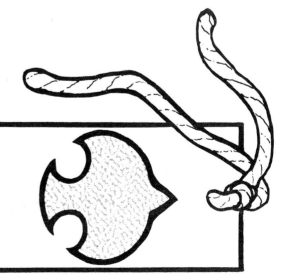

Signs and Symbols

BOOKMARKERS   Grades 1-8

Materials Needed:

Cardboard patterns of symbols
Lightweight posterboard
Colored construction paper
Crayons
Felt tip pens
Hand paper punch
Colored twine, yarn or ribbon
Clear contact paper

Before Class:

Prepare cardboard patterns for the students.

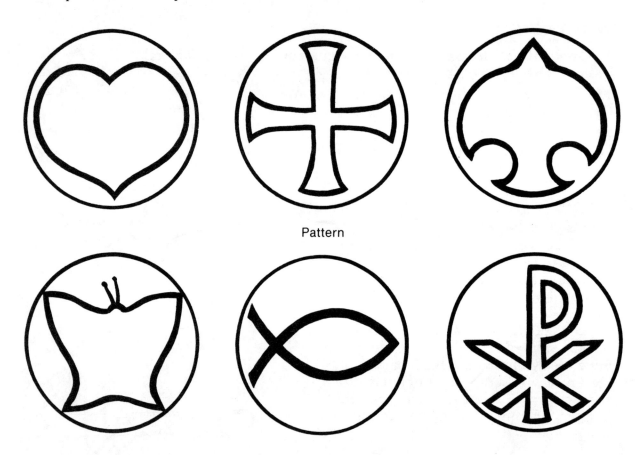

Pattern

Procedure:

1. This project may be done by using colored construction paper for the symbols and lightweight posterboard for the bookmarkers.
2. Choose one of the symbol patterns and trace it on a piece of construction paper.
3. Glue the symbol onto the posterboard bookmarker.
4. Decorate the bookmarker with crayons or felt tip pens. A Bible verse may be added.
5. Place finished bookmarker between two pieces of clear contact paper.
6. Punch a hole near the top and loop a piece of colored twine, yarn or narrow ribbon through the top of the bookmarker.

PUZZLE PROJECT   Grades 3-6

Materials Needed:

Magazines
Stiff cardboard (from pads of paper)
Glue
Scissors
White paper
Crayons
Drawing pencils

Procedure:

One important way to understand "Church" is to see it as community. We are the Church. From a magazine, cut out a picture of groups of people symbolizing community, or have the students draw a picture of their own family and community with different people in the picture.

Glue the picture to the stiff cardboard. Do not use corrugated cardboard. Turn the cardboard over and draw lines on the back to make a puzzle outline. Cut out the puzzle pieces following the lines. Students can trade puzzle pieces and work each others' puzzle.

COVERED CLIP BOOKMARKERS   Grades 5-8

Materials Needed:

Flat, metal spring type hairclip — one per student
Felt in a variety of colors — red, blue, green, white, yellow, etc.
Cardboard patterns of symbols
Pencils
White glue
Scissors
Wax paper

Optional: Trim material such as gold braid, silver and gold thread, embroidery floss, ribbon, etc.

Before Class:

Prepare ample cardboard patterns for the students.

Procedure:

1. Trace a pattern of choice four times on a piece of felt. Some students may wish to make their own pattern. Be sure each pattern will cover the hairclip with room to glue on the sides. Cut out the pieces.
2. Glue two pieces of felt around the top prong of the hair clip and glue the remaining two pieces of felt around the bottom prong of the hairclip.
3. Separate the two sets of felt with a piece of wax paper to prevent the clip from "gluing shut" while the glue is drying.
4. Decorate the top symbol with extra pieces of felt and/or trim. For example, if a symbol of the Bible is used, white felt could be cut to represent the pages of the Bible. If a chalice symbol is used, gold thread could be glued on the chalice in the shape of a cross.

Pattern

13

Church

FISH SYMBOL   Grades 1-4

Materials Needed:

Fish pattern for each student
Scissors
Glue
Sheet of fish scales for each student

Procedure:

1. Distribute a fish pattern to each student along with a sheet of fish scales representing the people-Church.
2. Have the students cut out all the fish scales and glue them onto the fish.
3. Explain to the students that the fish represents Jesus Christ, Son of God, Savior. The "scales" represent the people in community with Jesus, forming the Church.
4. Optional: Some students may want to draw faces on the fish scales.

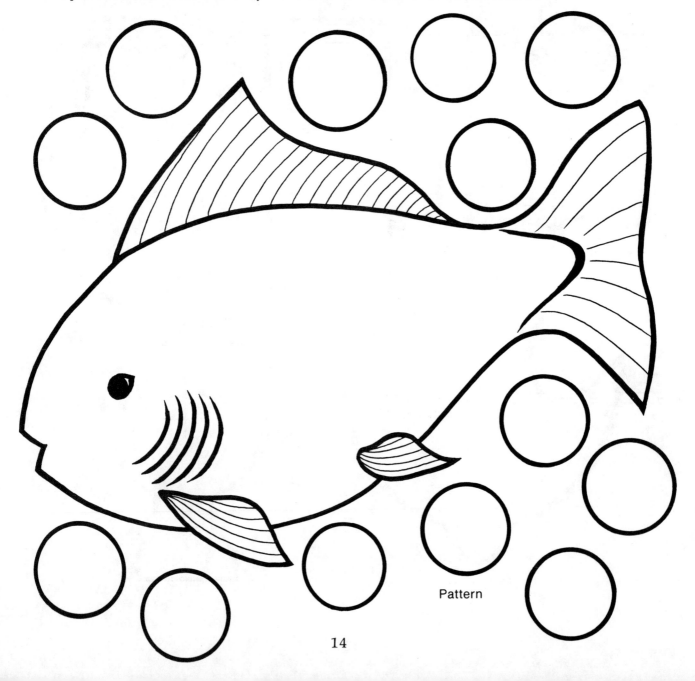

Pattern

Church

OUR ROOTS ART MURAL   Grades 1-8

Materials Needed:

Roll of white shelf paper or newsprint
Crayons or paint, brushes and newspapers

Procedure:

1. As a good review of the year, have the students reflect the story and heritage of the Church from Abraham and Joseph to the Church in the world today.
2. Have the students put their Church story in art form as a mural.
3. Encourage the students to include themselves as part of the Church in the world today.

SPLATTER PAINT CHURCH SYMBOLS   Grades 1-8

Materials Needed:

Cross and fish patterns
Straight pins to hold the pattern on the construction paper
Construction paper
Tempera paint
Piece of screen that has a fine mesh to it
Old toothbrushes or sponge or paint brush to force the paint through the screen
Newspapers
Optional: White shoe polish and a ruler

You may need teacher aides for this project.

Before Class:

Cut out a sample pattern of the cross or fish for each student.

Procedure:

1. Cover the work area with newspapers.
2. Fasten the pattern to the construction paper by putting straight pins straight up and down into the pattern and the construction paper.
3. The diagram shows how splatter painting is done. Dip the toothbrush into the tempera paint and then rub it over the screen wire.
4. Optional: You may also use white shoe polish and splatter it on by rubbing the toothbrush against the side of a ruler.

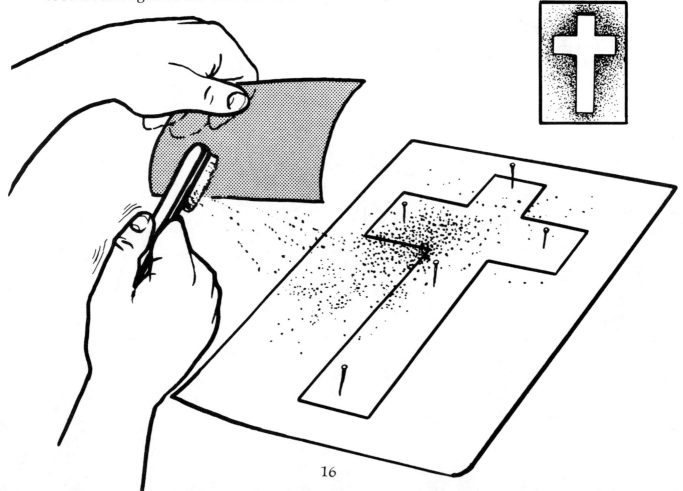

Pattern

Church

EMBOSSED PICTURE   Grades 4-8

Materials Needed:

4" square of embossing foil
Wood-grained paper plate
Ribbon
Pencil
Rubber cement
Tape
Knife
Paper
Scissors
Paper punch
Church symbol patterns
Cellophane

Procedure:

1. Trace a pattern of the church symbols on plain paper and lay it over the embossing foil. Tape the paper with the symbol on it and foil together.
2. Using a dull pencil, trace over the design so that the design is transferred to the foil.
3. Remove the pattern. With the same side up, trace over all the lines again so that they will be raised on the opposite side. Turn the foil over and use the eraser end of the pencil to rub in the area between the lines. With careful work and extra rubbing, the design can be made to stand out well from the background.
4. Make slits in the paper plate with a knife so the foil can be inserted into the slits at the corners.
5. Insert the corners of the foil into the paper plate. Apply the rubber cement to the corners to hold the foil in position. Punch a hole at the top of the paper plate. Slip a ribbon through the hole and tie the ribbon in a bow, leaving a loop for hanging.

Pattern

Church

PEOPLE COLLAGE   Grades 1-8

Materials Needed:

Old magazines
Scissors
Glue
Colored construction paper
Magic markers
Rulers
Pencils

Procedure:

1. From old magazines, cut different faces of people.
2. Glue the faces to a large piece of construction paper.
3. Print "We are the Church" at the top for Grades 1 and 2. (Younger children may do the printing themselves if they are able.)
4. Direct the older children to arrange the faces in a shape or symbol that represents "Church." They may draw their own symbol or drawing of a church first and then arrange the faces inside the symbol. (See sample idea.)
5. Cut out the symbol containing the faces and glue it to a larger piece of construction paper of a contrasting color.
6. Print "We are the Church" on the larger construction paper.

Baptism

WALNUT SAIL BOAT   Grades 1-2

Materials Needed:

Walnut half for each student
Round toothpicks
Florist clay
Construction paper
White glue

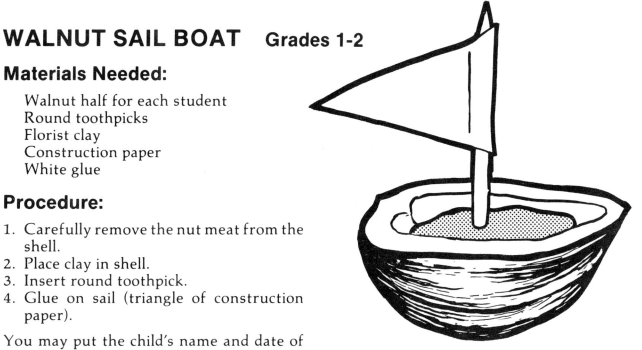

Procedure:

1. Carefully remove the nut meat from the shell.
2. Place clay in shell.
3. Insert round toothpick.
4. Glue on sail (triangle of construction paper).

You may put the child's name and date of Baptism on the sail before you glue the sail onto the toothpick. Or the students may put their names and Baptism dates on the sails when they get home.

Baptism

WALNUT BOAT MOBILE   Grades 5-8

Materials Needed:

Five walnut shell halves per student
Two 12" sticks per student
Hard plastic foam
Round toothpicks
Paper sails from construction paper
White glue
Thread or fishing line

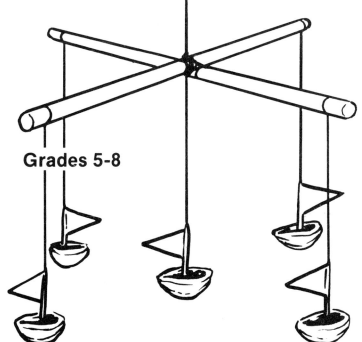

Procedure:

1. Cross the two sticks together and tie them securely at the center joint.
2. Glue a piece of foam to the inside of each walnut half.
3. Glue a toothpick, with a sail attached, to the center of the foam to make a walnut boat. Repeat this four more times.
4. Tie threads to toothpick tops and add a dash of glue to keep thread from slipping. Tie one walnut boat to each end of the 12" sticks. Tie one boat from the center joint.

Baptism

BAPTISM MOBILE   Grades 1-4

Materials Needed:

Cardboard
Mobile patterns of baptismal symbols
Scissors
Construction paper
Thread or yarn
Glue
Cellophane tape
Coat hanger
Paper punch

You may need teacher aides for this project.

Before Class:

Fold a large piece of blue construction paper in half to make the water symbol which will be used to encase the hanger. At the open end of the construction paper, draw and cut out waves. Glue the water symbol at the top of the waves and around the hanger. Prepare sets of baptismal symbols on cardboard for the students to trace.

Procedure:

1. Have the students trace the cardboard symbols onto construction paper.
2. Cut out the symbols.
3. Punch a hole in each symbol.
4. Using tape or glue, attach yarn or thread in different lengths to the symbols.
5. Hang the candle, robe, and oil symbols from the water symbol.
6. Loop a piece of yarn or thread through the top of the water frame for hanging.
7. Tie symbols in various lengths to water symbol (hanger).

Pattern

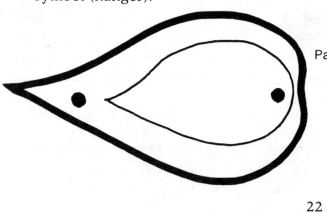

22

BAPTISM MOBILE   Grades 5-8

Materials Needed:

Symbols of Baptism
Cardboard
String or yarn
Scissors
Paper punch
Colored tissue paper: blue for water, yellow for oil, gold or orange for the candle, white for the garment

Procedure:

1. Have the students cut out the enclosed symbols for the sacrament of Baptism.
2. Cut two patterns for each symbol in order to glue them together later.
3. Cut out the center of each of the symbols, leaving an opening in the middle for tissue paper.
4. Use different colored tissue papers to decorate and accentuate the insides of the symbols.
5. Glue tissue paper to one of the symbols and then place its twin on the top.
6. Reinforce the water symbol on the hanger itself with a strip of cardboard at the bottom. Then hang the other symbols from the water symbol.

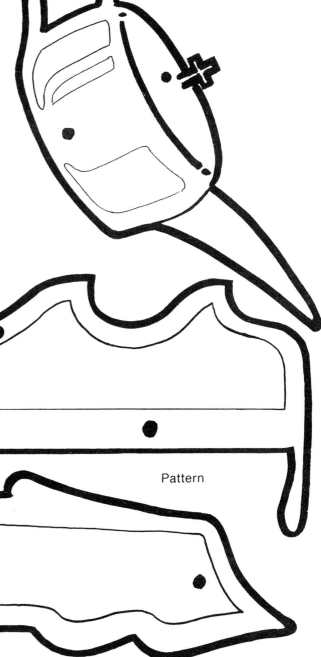

Pattern

Baptism

CANDLEMAKING   Grades 3-8

Materials Needed:

Partly used candles or parafin wax
Old crayons
Coffee cans or pans in which to melt wax
Small milk cartons
Cupcake molds or other waxed containers (style and size of container depends on the kind and size of candle you want to make)
Heavy white string
Scissors
Pan
Knife

For grades 3 and 4, you may want teacher aides for this project.

Procedure:

1. Melt old candles or parafin in a pan or in a coffee can over very low heat.
2. Sliver old crayons to color the wax. Stir into the melting wax.
3. Cut or shape molds, if necessary.
4. Cut string into lengths for wicks at least 3 inches longer than the candle will be. Tie a knot on one end of the string. Soak the string in melted parafin. Stretch the string out straight to harden.

5. Puncture bottom of the container and thread the waxed string through it. To hold in the center, place a stick or pencil across the top of the container and wrap the wick around it. Stand the containers in a pan and completely fill each container with melted wax. Allow to harden. This will take at least overnight. Larger candles take from 5 to 18 hours to harden. When completely hard, peel off the container from the candle. Scrape off pieces with a knife.

Floating Candles:

Floating candles are made by using paper cupcake molds. The waxed wicks are inserted when the wax is almost hard. This will keep the wick straight.

Another Idea for Candles:

Drip various colors of wax over the already hardened candles or over ready-made candles.

Baptism

BAPTISM CANDLE Grades 1-4

Materials Needed:

Votive candle or inexpensive white taper for each student
Glue
Sequins or glitter

Procedure:

1. Give each of the students one candle. Tell them that this candle represents the baptismal candle.
2. Have the students decorate the candle with different colored sequins or roll the candles in glitter.
3. When the students take their candles home, the candles will need to be put in candle holders. Suggest that the students use this candle for special family celebrations or light it for prayer at mealtime.

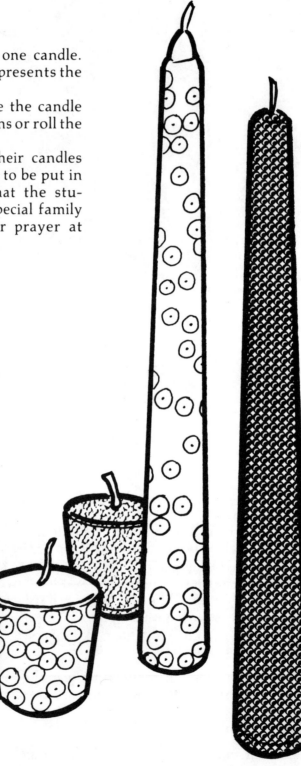

Baptism

PAINTED SEA SHELLS   Grades 3-8

Materials Needed:

Clean sea shells
Tempera paint
Liquid soap
Brushes
Newspapers
Containers for the paint

Procedure:

1. Mix a few drops of liquid soap into the tempera paint. This helps the paint stick to the shell.
2. Have the students paint their name and date of Baptism on the outside of the shell.
3. Have the students paint an appropriate scene on the inside of the shell.

Baptism

SHELL MOBILE   Grades 5-8

Materials Needed:

Clean sea shells with a small hole drilled in at the top of each one (5 shells per student)
Fishing line or thread
Tempera paint
Liquid soap
Brushes
Newspapers
Two 12″ sticks
Glue
Scissors
Containers for the paint

Procedure:

1. Mix a few drops of liquid soap into the tempera paint This helps the paint stick to the shell.
2. On the shells, paint the different symbols or signs used for Baptism.
3. Cross the two 12″ sticks together and tie them securely at the center joint.
4. Tie fishing line or thread to each shell and hang the shells from the four ends of the crossed sticks. The fifth shell can be hung from the center point.

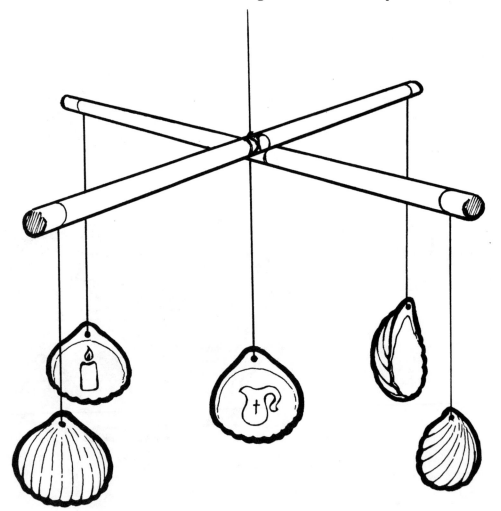

Confirmation

PERSONAL QUALITIES BOX   Grades 6-8

This project will allow students to express and reveal their inner qualities as well as their visible qualities by choosing pictures and/or key words to show the progression from outward appearances to inner realities. Instruct the students to cover the exterior of the box with pictures and words to show what they like to do and how they perceive their ideal selves by what they wish for themselves. Instruct the students to use pictures and words to reveal their inner selves by showing some of their hidden qualities such as a sense of humor, shyness, tenderness, etc. An alternative would be to show the stages of development of the student from infancy to childhood to adolescence, according to the age of the student.

Materials Needed:

Box with a lid — one per student
White latex paint
Magazine pictures and/or magazines
Drawing instruments (crayons, magic markers, water color paints)
Glue
Newspapers
Paint brushes
Scissors

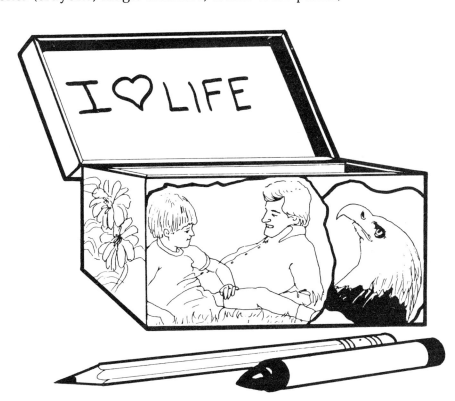

Before Class:

Unless the boxes are new, you may wish to paint the boxes and lids inside and outside with white latex paint. If you do this before class, proceed to #2.

Procedure:

1. Have the students paint the boxes and lids inside and outside with white latex paint. Let dry.
2. Using magazine pictures, have the students glue pictures onto the box which reveal the students' own inner selves.
3. Students may use quotes from poems, prayers, advertisements or their own words to caption their creations. Allow options and exploration.

Confirmation

PINWHEELS   Grades 1-4

The wind is an idea that can help us understand the presence of the Holy Spirit. The Bible speaks of the Holy Spirit in symbols of fire and wind. The wind cannot be seen and yet the effect of the wind is very real to us. The Holy Spirit is God's presence with us. As the students make the pinwheels and watch them turn with the wind, remind the students that the Holy Spirit is moving in their hearts.

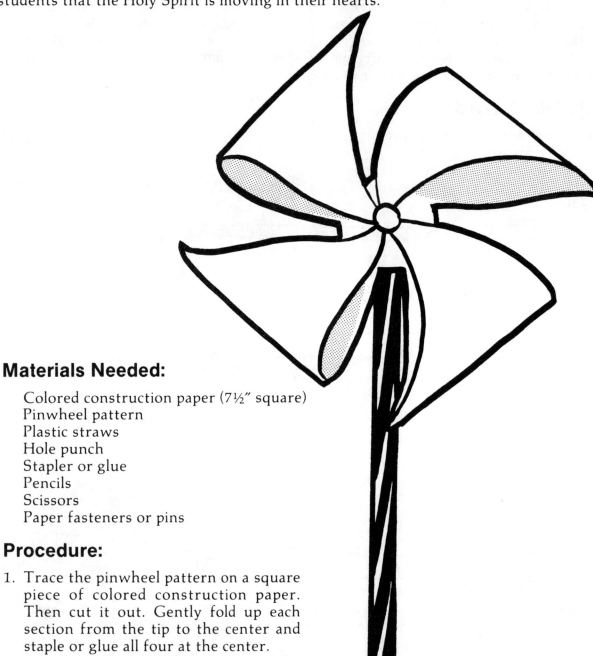

Materials Needed:

Colored construction paper (7½" square)
Pinwheel pattern
Plastic straws
Hole punch
Stapler or glue
Pencils
Scissors
Paper fasteners or pins

Procedure:

1. Trace the pinwheel pattern on a square piece of colored construction paper. Then cut it out. Gently fold up each section from the tip to the center and staple or glue all four at the center.
2. Punch a hole through the center of the pinwheel and through the top of the straw in order to insert a paper fastener through both items. Spread the paper fastener's prongs on the backside of the straw to secure it in place. Pins may be substituted for fasteners.

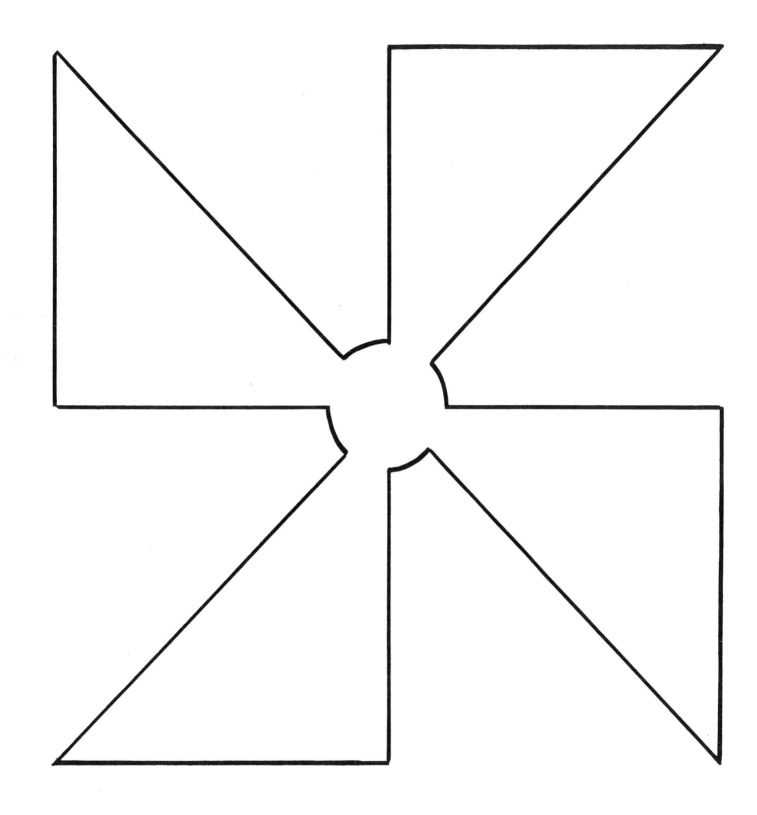

Pattern

HOLY SPIRIT MOBILE   Grades 1-8

Materials Needed:

Cardboard pattern of Holy Spirit mobile pieces
White posterboard
Red construction paper
White yarn or string
Scissors
Pencils
Paper punch
Stapler or cellophane tape
Small plastic ring (optional)

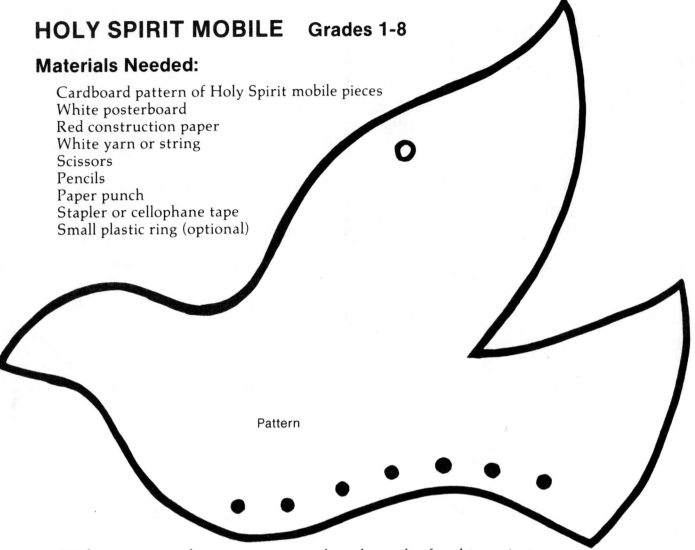

Pattern

With younger students, you may need teacher aides for this project.

Before Class:

Prepare adequate numbers of cardboard patterns for the Holy Spirit mobile. For each of the younger students, you may wish to pre-cut the dove symbol out of the white posterboard. Mark with a small "x" where the student should punch out the holes. Then proceed to step #3 during class.

Procedure:

1. Trace dove pattern on the white posterboard. Mark with an "x" where the holes should go.
2. Cut out the dove and punch out the holes.
3. Trace seven "tongues of fire" or flames on the red construction paper and cut them out.
4. Tie various lengths (6"-12" long) of yarn from the Holy Spirit dove symbol.
5. Staple or tape one flame to each length of yarn.
6. Tie one 8" length of yarn to the top of the dove. Make a loop and tie it into a knot in order to hang up the mobile. You might want to tie a small plastic ring to the top in order to hang up the mobile.
7. Optional: Have the students write a gift of the Holy Spirit (Wisdom, Knowledge, Faith, Prayer, Courage, Hope or Love) on each flame.

HOLY SPIRIT MOBILE Grades 5-8

Materials Needed:

Lightweight cardboard pattern of dove — one per student
Cardboard pattern of "tongues of fire" (flame) — one per student
White felt
Red felt
White yarn or string
White glue
Scissors
Pencils
Small plastic ring — one per student
Paper punch

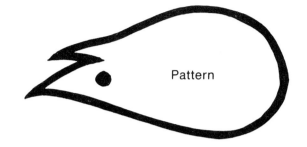

Before Class:

Prepare cardboard patterns of dove and "tongues of fire" (flame). Make a sample mobile.

Procedure:

1. Using the cardboard patterns, trace two doves on the white felt.
2. Cut out and glue the two felt doves onto the cardboard dove — one on each side. (With cardboard "sandwiched" in the middle, the dove is made more durable.)
3. Set aside to dry.
4. Trace the "tongues of fire" (flame) pattern on the red felt seven times.
5. Cut out and punch a hole near the top of each flame.
6. Punch seven holes along the bottom of the dove and one hole on top for hanging. (See pattern for placement of holes.)
7. Tie one piece of yarn approximately 7" long to the top of the dove. Tie the other end of the yarn to the plastic ring for hanging.
8. Using different lengths of white yarn, tie and hang the flames from the dove so that the mobile is balanced.

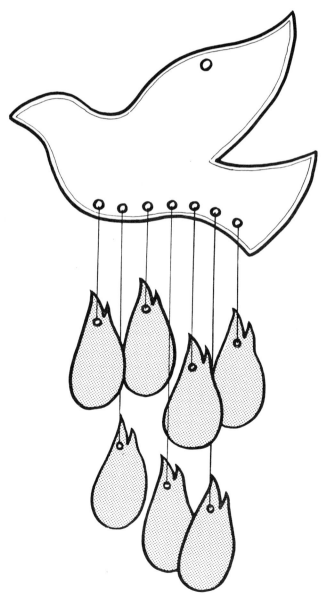

NAME PLAQUE   Grades 5-8

This project affirms the student's identity as a child of God who has been called by name as very special and precious to God.

The resource book, *What's In A Name?* by Linda Frances, John Hartzell and Al Palmquist (ARK Products, Minneapolis, MN, 1976), contains over 700 names and their meanings. It gives the "literal" meaning of a name and a suggested character quality with an appropriate scripture verse. This is a different approach from secular name books.

Some names may be difficult to find. You may have to use other name books that give the meaning of a name or you can give students a positive characteristic that you have observed in them, such as faithfulness, a gentle spirit, truthfulness, etc. Give each student a special Bible verse that will strengthen the student.

This is a two-part project. Students prepare names in one session and finish the plaque in the next session.

Materials Needed:

8" x 6" piece of wood per student
Sandpaper
Permanent markers in fine points and wide
Pencils
Rulers
White Glue
What's In A Name? book or a book with meanings of names
Book of Saints
Bible
Spray varnish
Picture hanger

Before Class:

Look up each student's name. Prepare the meaning of each name or the characteristic you have observed. Type or print an appropriate Bible verse on a white piece of paper. This will be glued to the bottom section of the plaque.

Procedure:

1. Cover the table and floor with newspaper and sand the wood until it is smooth.
2. Have the students practice designing their own first name on scrap paper.
3. Draw lines (1 to 1½" high) lightly in pencil on the wood for the name. ½" below the name put the meaning of the name (½" high). Leave a space of ½" between the name and its meaning. Arrange the meaning of name or characteristic in a ½" space.
4. Lightly pencil in name in the top 1 to 1½" space. Try to center it, allowing space for wide marker.
5. Skip the next ½" space.
6. Using pencil, lightly write in characteristic or meaning of name in the ½" space. Center carefully. You will use the fine point marker for this part.
7. Trace over the pencil lines with markers. Use wide markers for the top name. Use fine point markers for characteristic of the name.
8. Glue scripture verse to the bottom of the plaque.
9. Spray or varnish plaques in a well-ventilated area.
10. When dry, add picture hangers to the back.

35

Eucharist

HAND COOKIES Grades 1-4

When we come together to celebrate the liturgy we share bread. It is important that we share with others so that we are generous and loving people who are concerned about other people. The hand cookies that we will be making can show how we are God's helpers in the world.

Materials Needed:

Recipe:
    ½ cup shortening (½ butter or margarine, softened)
    1 cup sugar
    1 egg
    1 tsp. baking powder
    1 tsp. vanilla
    2 2/3 cup flour
    ½ tsp. soda
    ½ tsp. salt
    ¼ tsp. nutmeg
    ½ cup dairy sour cream

Oven
Pastry wheel
Cookie sheet
Mixing bowl and spoon
Rolling pin
Mixes

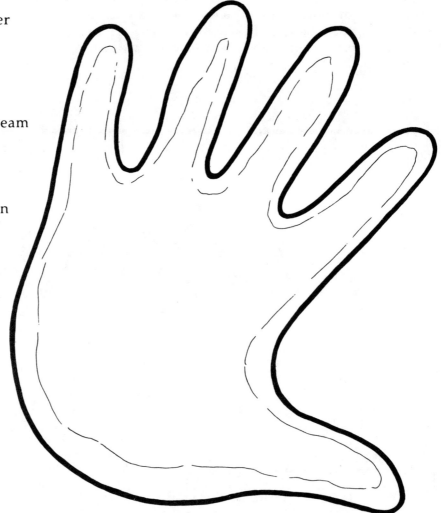

Procedure:

Heat oven to 425°. Mix shortening, sugar, egg and vanilla. Blend in remaining ingredients. Divide dough into three parts. Roll each part ¼" thick on floured surface. Trace around the student's hand with a pastry wheel. Form any remaining dough into desired shapes. Bake 6 to 8 minutes. Cool. Decorate as desired. Makes about 6 hand cookies and 1 dozen 2" cookies.

Eucharist

STORYBLOCK Grades 1-4

Materials Needed:

Lightweight cardboard
Block pattern
White glue
Scissors
Crayons or drawing pencils

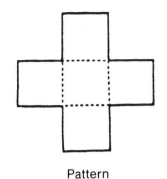

Pattern

Before Class:

Make ample block patterns for your class to use.

Procedure:

1. Make the pattern for the block to resemble the one in the sketch. Dimensions may vary as long as the sections are square.
2. Trace the pattern twice on the lightweight cardboard. Cut out the two pieces.
3. Fold up on the outside sections of each piece. Glue one half of the block inside the other half of the block.
4. Decorate each side of the block with pictures which symbolize the Eucharist, the Last Supper or ways people nourish each other spiritually and/or physically.

Pattern

Eucharist

LACED PICTURE PLAQUE   Grades 1-4

Materials Needed:

Paper plates with holes to use as cardboard circles
Construction paper
Yarn
Artificial flowers or nature materials such as acorn caps, unusual small stones, seeds, etc.
Paper punch
White glue
Crayons
Pencils
Scissors

You may need aides for this project.

Before Class:

Punch holes equidistant around the outside of the paper plate about one-fourth inch from the edge.

Procedure:

1. On the construction paper, have the students color symbols of the Eucharist. You may provide symbols to trace or the students may draw their own.
2. After the students have colored their symbols, the symbols should be cut out.
3. Glue the Eucharist symbol in the center of the circle. Glue artificial flowers or other materials on the circle to decorate around the Eucharist symbol.
4. Lace yarn through the holes around the circle. (Allow enough lacing at the beginning and the end to tie for hanging.)

Eucharist

BAKER'S CLAY MAGNETS   Grades 1-8

Materials Needed:

Baker's Clay (see recipe below)
Magnet strips
Aluminum foil
Cookie sheets
For Rolling Pin Method: rolling pins and tools (e.g. cookie cutters, forks, table knife, pencils, paper clips, toothpicks)

Baker's Clay Recipe: 1½ c. hot water, 1 c. salt, 4 c. flour. Mix salt and hot water in a large bowl. Add flour and mix until sticky. Knead the dough until smooth (about 7-10 minutes). If dough is too crumbly, add a few drops of water. If dough is too sticky, add more flour. Seal in a heavy plastic bag and store in the refrigerator until ready to use.

Note: These clay magnets have to be baked and returned to the students at their next session. For the younger students, you may need aides.

40

Before Class:

Make up a sufficient amount of Baker's Clay. This clay can be made a few days in advance and stored in a tight plastic container in the refrigerator.

Procedure:

1. Give each student a small piece of Baker's Clay and a piece of aluminum foil on which to work.
2. By pinching and pulling, have the students shape the clay into a miniature loaf of bread, one slice of bread or a biscuit.
3. Place on a cookie sheet and bake in 300° oven for about 1½ hours. (Turn once.) Cool.
4. You may spray both sides of the "bread creations" with polyurethane varnish after they are baked and before you return them to the students. Instead, the students could "paint" their bread dough creations with two to three coats of clear nail polish.
5. Add a magnetic strip to the back of the dough creation. You may wish to attach a scripture verse.
6. Have the students take the magnets home and place them on the refrigerator. Students could make extras for gifts.

Rolling Pin Method: Roll out dough to ½" thick. (Do this on aluminum foil.) Use cookie cutters (heart shape to represent love, etc.) or have the students cut out various shapes with a table knife. To add clay details, moisten the pieces with a small amount of water to make the clay stick together. To imprint, use tools such as pencils, paper clips or toothpicks to "draw" a cross symbol on the bread creation.

Optional: Roll Baker's Clay into long snakes and form Christian symbols (Chi Rho, cross, dove, etc.). Complete the process by following steps #3 through #6 listed above.

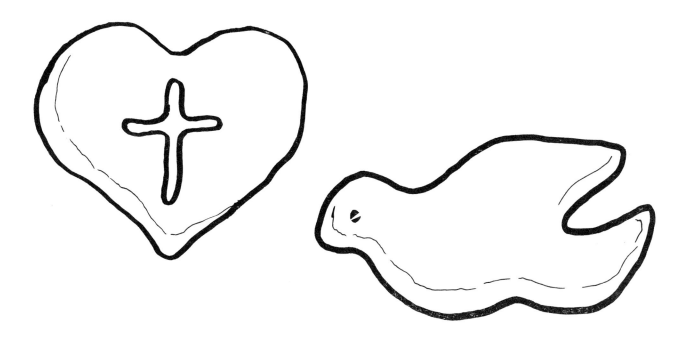

"LOVE" BREAD FEAST   Grades 1-8

Materials Needed:

Oven
Your favorite bread recipe (or prepared muffin dough that comes in refrigerator tubes)
Muffin tins
Napkins
Optional: butter and jelly, knife and spoon

Before Class:

Prepare the bread dough and let it rise (or buy sufficient tubes of muffin dough).

Procedure:

1. Give each student a piece of bread dough to knead.
2. Place each piece of dough in a greased muffin tin and bake 7-10 minutes.
3. When the muffins are done, say a thanksgiving prayer to Jesus and let each student eat his or her muffin. (Serve muffins with butter or jelly if desired.)
4. You may wish to make extra pieces so the students can bring home the bread they baked to share with someone in their family.

Grades 5-8: You may wish to have the students roll out the dough into long snakes and form into Christian symbols such as Chi Rho, cross, dove, etc.

Eucharist

CELEBRATION FLAT BREAD   Grades 5-8

Materials Needed:

Recipe:
   6 Tbs. margarine or butter
   1 tsp. salt
   3 cups flour
   1½ cups chopped onion (optional)
   ¾ cup warm water

Copy of recipe for each group of students
Stove
Iron skillet or frying pan for each group
Mixing bowl and spoon
Spatulas
Cooling racks

Procedure:

1. Have students work in small groups. Adults should be in charge of frying the bread for the students.
2. Melt 1 Tbsp. margarine in pan and saute onions until transparent (not brown) for about 1-2 minutes (optional).
3. If you are not using onions, melt 6 Tbsp. margarine or butter. Put melted margarine or butter into a mixing bowl. Add water, salt, and 2½ cups flour. Mix together. Add ½ cup flour or less so that mixture is not sticky to work with.
4. Form into balls and divide into 16 pieces. Roll each into 8" circles.
5. Preheat ungreased iron skillet. Skillet is ready when a drop of water placed in the skillet evaporates immediately. Fry each circle about 3-4 minutes, turning once. Bread will not brown evenly. Cool on racks. Serve while still warm.

Reconciliation

COLORING WITH YARN CROSS   Grades 1-4

Materials Needed:

Posterboard (approximately 5" x 8") — 1 per student
Colored yarn
Scissors
Newspaper
White glue
Paper punch
Ruler
Optional activity: Burlap, pencil or chalk, wax paper, dowel rod

Before Class:

Cut the posterboard. Cut yarn into 12" lengths for grades 1 and 2. Punch holes in the top of the cross and add yarn in order to hang the cross.

Procedure:

1. Have the students draw a large simple cross on their posterboard. (Check to see that it is large enough.) The students may use a ruler if they wish.
2. Cut a piece of yarn about 12" in length.
3. Spread glue on the vertical bar of the cross.
4. Take yarn and, starting with the outside edge of the cross, press the yarn gently to the posterboard, spiraling inward. Trim excess yarn or add more until all the cross area is filled in.
5. Fill in the horizontal bar of the cross in the same manner. You may do the two sides separately or glue yarn right over the vertical bar.
6. To hang, punch two holes near the top of the posterboard and string a piece of yarn through them. Make a knot behind each hole to secure the yarn.

Optional: You may also "draw" this yarn cross on a piece of burlap.

Sketch the cross onto the burlap with pencil or chalk. Use a piece of wax paper underneath the burlap. Then when the glue is applied it won't leak through and stick to the newspaper on the table. Follow procedures #2 through #5 from above. Glue the burlap onto a dowel rod to hang.

GOOD DEED TREE   Grades 1-4

Materials Needed:

Leafless tree branch
Coffee can full of sand
Yarn
Gift wrap paper
Glue
Paper punch

You may need one or two aides for this project.

Procedure:

1. Cover a coffee can with decorative paper.
2. Set the branch down into the sand to hold the branch upright.
3. Have the students make little booklets from gift wrapping paper and write the promise of a good deed inside each booklet. (One or two aides will be needed to help the younger students write their good deeds.)
4. Punch a hole in each booklet. Using yarn, tie the booklet to the tree.
5. Help the students remember to do their good deeds by suggesting they make a "promise" tree at home.
6. This project can be brought to the liturgy and presented as the students' gift.

LEATHER-LOOK TWIG CROSS   Grades 3-8

Materials Needed:

Newspapers
Masking tape
Brown shoe polish
Old rags
Twigs — 2 per student
Optional: Wire, shellac, brushes

Procedure:

1. Wire or tape two twigs together to form a cross.
2. Cover twigs completely with masking tape.
3. Rub brown shoe polish over all the masking tape.
4. Use an old rag to wipe off the extra polish.
5. Shellac the cross. (optional)

More Ideas for Crosses:

Fabric cross: Cut a scrap of fabric material into the shape of a cross. Glue the cross to a piece of posterboard, burlap or felt. (Grades 1-2)

Wallpaper cross: Use old sample wallpaper books. Pick out a wallpaper design. (Small prints look fine.) Cut the wallpaper into the shape of a cross. Glue the cross to burlap, felt or posterboard. (Grades 1-2)

A Bible verse could be added to any of the crosses by gluing it to the bottom or top of the cross.

NEEDLEPOINT CROSS   Grades 5-8

This age group enjoys learning how to do needlepoint. Work in small groups of three or four students. Recruit some needlepoint crafters from your parish to assist you. This is an excellent opportunity for some of the elderly who do needlepoint to get involved. (This project may take two sessions.)

Materials Needed:

#7 plastic canvas, 2¼″ wide by 3″ long — 1 per student
Needlepoint needles — 1 per student
Light and dark colored yarn in a variety of colors
Scissors

Before Class:

Give each aide a copy of the instructions. Have the aides make samples for the class in advance of the session. You may wish to have the yarn cut into 18″ lengths.

Procedure:

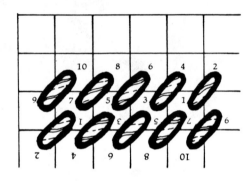

1. Divide the class into small groups of three or four students. Assign an aide to each group.
2. Have the students pick out two colors of yarn.
3. Have an aide pass out a plastic canvas and needle to each student.
4. Each group may now proceed at its own pace.

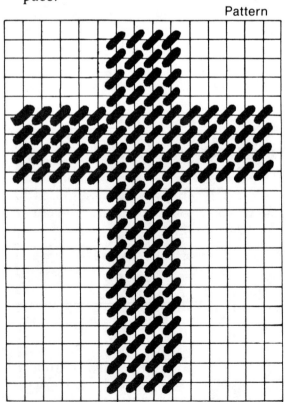

Pattern

Instructions:

The cross design can be worked in a dark colored yarn and the background in a contrasting or lighter color.

Continental Stitch: Start design at upper right corner. To begin, hold an inch of yarn in back and work over this end. All other strands may be started and finished by running them through the wrong side of the finished work.

Work with yarn about 18″ long. Bring the needle up at 1. Go down at 2 diagonally across one mesh of the canvas (see diagram). The needle comes up again at 3, one mesh to the left of 1. Work in this manner to the end of the row. Turn canvas around and work back. Work "right" to "left."

The edges may be trimmed smooth with a scissors. The edges may be whip stitched for a more finished look. Tie a piece of yarn at the top two corners to make a hanger.

Reconciliation

CHURCH WINDOWS   Grades 5-8

Materials Needed:

Sponges
Tempera paint (yellow-green and blue-green)
White posterboard (any size)
Black paper
White paper
White glue
Black felt tip pen

"He was lost
and is found"
—Luke 15:32

Procedure:

Note: Leave a space at the bottom of the posterboard for printing a Scripture passage.

1. Dip the sponge into bright yellow-green tempera paint and pat all over the white posterboard. Repeat with a deeper blue-green paint, shading heavier in the center.
2. Cut two identical church window frames from the pattern provided, one black and one white frame, and fasten with glue over the shaded background.
3. Have the students find Scripture readings from those taught in the Scripture class. Using felt tip pens, print a passage on the bottom of the picture.

Pattern

49

Anointing of the Sick

GIFT BOOKLETS   Grades 1-4

The Scripture booklet makes an excellent gift for any shut-in or hospital patient. Give the joke booklet to someone who is well enough to enjoy it.

Remind the students that the Sacrament of the Anointing of the Sick is the Church's sign of its concern for the sick and elderly. This gift booklet is the students' sign of concern. Have the students share their booklets with someone they know who is sick or elderly.

Materials Needed:

Construction paper
Flower seals or pictures from magazines
Scripture verses, jokes, inspirational poems cut from magazines
Yarn
Scissors
Felt pens
Glue
Paper punch

Before Class:

1. Cut construction paper into sections of 9" x 6". Use two sections folded in half for each booklet.
2. With a paper punch, punch holes in the fold.

Procedure:

1. Pull yarn through the punched holes and tie the yarn in a bow in the outside fold of the booklet.
2. Paste a flower picture on the cover and then alternate pasting flowers and Scripture verses on each of the inside pages to make a Scripture booklet.
3. For a joke booklet, paste a cartoon or several printed jokes on each page. Decorate the remainder of each page with smiling faces drawn with felt tip pens.

AIR FRESHENER BALL   Grades 1-4

Remind the students of the meaning of the Sacrament of the Anointing of the Sick and have the students give this gift as a sign of their concern for the sick and elderly.

Materials Needed:

Orange — 1 per student
Whole cloves
Narrow ribbon
Straight pins

You may need aides to help the students tie the ribbon.

Procedure:

1. Use a fairly large, firm orange. Insert the cloves until the surface is covered and the fruit looks like a porcupine.
2. Tie two narrow pieces of ribbon around the orange, fastening firmly on the top.
3. Attach a ribbon cluster at the top and make a loop for hanging.
4. The air freshener ball may be hung in a closet or placed in a shoe container.

SCRIPTURAL BOUQUET   Grades 1-4

Materials Needed:

Fresh or artificial flowers
Paper
Pencils
Ribbon
Scripture verses for the students to copy
Scissors
Paper punch
Small jars such as jelly jars, baby food jars or mustard jars
Gift wrap
Styrofoam or sand to anchor flowers

You may need aides for this project to help the younger students write the Scripture verses.

Before Class:

Cut two strips of 2" x 8" paper for each student.

Procedure:

1. Have the students bring flowers from home.
2. Decorate small jars with gift wrap to make the vase.
3. Have the students choose and write a Scripture verse on each strip of paper.
4. Fold the paper twice and punch a hole in it. Using the ribbon, tie the papers to the flower.
5. Anchor the flowers by putting a small piece of styrofoam or sand in the bottom of the jar.

Anointing of the Sick

SACHET BALL   Grades 1-8

Materials Needed:

Newspapers
Aluminum tea ball
Brush and paint
Cotton
Perfume or powder sachet
Artificial flowers
Sequins, glitter, buttons
Doily sections
Gold cord

You may wish to have aides with this project for the younger students.

Procedure:

1. Paint the tea ball.
2. Fill the tea ball with the cotton and sprinkle the cotton with a few drops of perfume or sachet.
3. Decorate the ball with flowers, sequins, buttons, doily sections, glitter, etc. (Keep in mind the age of the students involved and use materials that are easily handled by them.)
4. As an option for the younger students, you could have the students tie colored ribbons around flowers and hang the flowers from under the lid of the tea ball.

Note: This sachet ball can be given as a gift to a resident in a senior citizen's home or to another senior citizen. Explain to the students that the Sacrament of the Anointing of the Sick is the Church's sign of concern for the sick and elderly. This gift is the students' sign of concern.

MARRIAGE RINGS COLLAGE   Grades 1-4

Materials Needed:

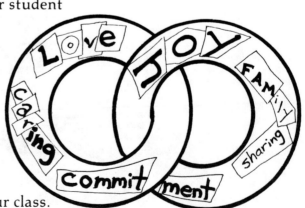

Cardboard, approximately 8″ square — 2 per student
Pencils
Glue or paste
Newspapers
Cellophane tape
Ring pattern
Old magazines
Scissors

You may need aides for the younger students.

Before Class:

Cut out an ample supply of patterns for your class. You may want to trace the pattern on the cardboard and cut it out for the younger students.

Procedure:

1. Trace the ring pattern twice on the cardboard pieces. Cut out the two rings.
2. Using the magazines, cut out pictures that show various aspects of a marriage. You might find some of the following: a young couple at a movie or picnic, a wedding ceremony, a couple eating dinner, a couple at their child's baptism, an older couple walking together, etc.
3. Put newspapers on the working surface and then glue the pictures in a collage onto the two rings. Let dry.
4. Cut one of the rings and intertwine it with the other, taping it back together again afterwards.

MARRIAGE RINGS COLLAGE   Grades 5-8

Materials Needed:

Cardboard, approximately 8″ square — 2 per student
Pencils
Glue or paste
Cellophane tape
Old magazines
Scissors
Newspapers
Gold foil or yellow construction paper
Ring pattern

Before Class:

Cut out an ample supply of patterns for your class.

Procedure:

1. Trace the ring pattern twice on the cardboard pieces. Cut out the two rings.
2. Trace the ring pattern twice on the gold foil or yellow construction paper. Cut out the two rings.
3. Glue the foil or construction rings onto the cardboard rings.
4. Using the magazines and newspapers, cut out letters and make words that show various elements of marriage. (The letters that make up the words should be of various colors, sizes and print styles.)
5. Glue the letters onto the rings. Some words you might end up with are: love, commitment, joy, sharing, caring, etc.
6. Cut one of the rings and intertwine it with the other, taping it back together again afterwards.

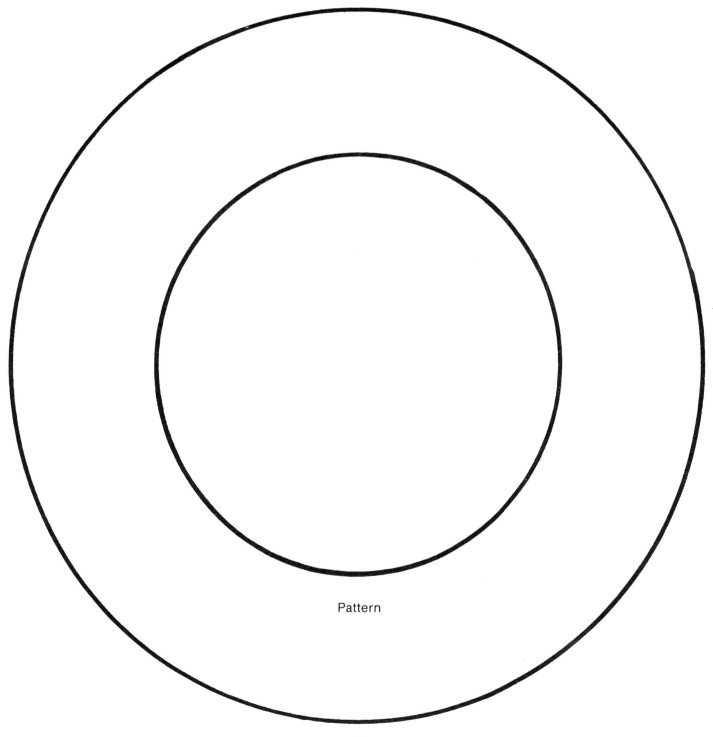

Pattern

Holy Orders

PRIESTHOOD MURAL   Grades 1-8

Materials Needed:

Roll of white shelf paper or newsprint
Crayons, markers or paints and paintbrushes
Newspapers

Procedure:

1. If using paints, cover the work surface with newspapers.
2. Have the students draw scenes that reflect the ministries of a priest. Some areas to cover are: administration of the sacraments, ministry to the elderly, hospital work, campus ministry, teaching, etc.

Sacraments/Sacramentals

MURAL   Grades 1-8

Materials Needed:

Roll of white shelf paper or newsprint
Crayons
Paint or magic markers

Procedure:

Have the students draw symbols of the sacraments and/or sacramentals. Hang the mural on the wall or hang it at a liturgical celebration on the final class day.

Faith

STORM AND CALM SEA PICTURE   Grades 1-4

Materials Needed:

Construction paper — light blue, medium blue, black, white, yellow
Ruler
Picture patterns
Glue
Pencils
Scissors

Procedure:

1. Trace and cut out the sections for the picture from construction paper, using the water, lightning, boat, cloud and sun patterns. Use light blue paper for water, white paper for the white cloud and boat, yellow paper for the sun and lightning and black paper for the black cloud.
2. For the background, take a full sheet of medium blue construction paper. Make a 3½" fold down from one of the narrow sides.
3. Glue the boat on the water at the bottom of the blue background.
4. Beneath the flap, glue the black cloud and lightning. Fold down the top flap and glue the white cloud and sun in place on the top flap.
5. Use the picture with the story about faith found in Matthew 8:23.

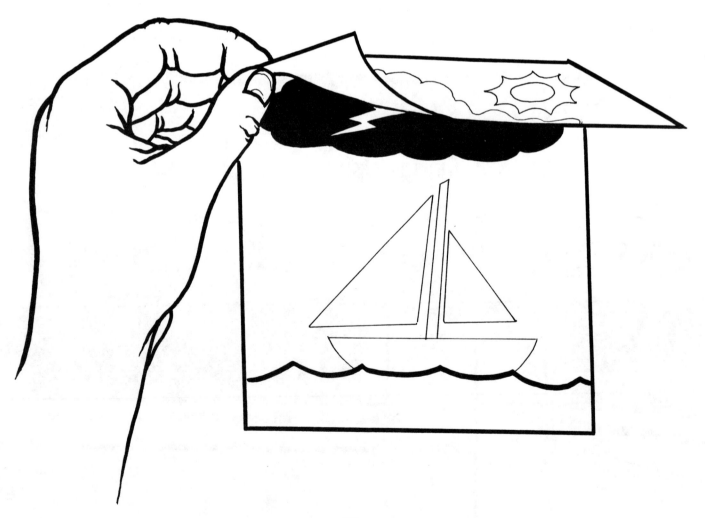

Pattern

Faith

CALM/STORMY SEA PICTURE   Grades 1-4

Materials Needed:

Typing paper
Light blue construction paper
Paper fastener
Crayons or colored chalk
Spray fixative for chalk
Scissors
Pencils

Procedure:

Begin this project by reading Matthew 8:23 or by telling the story in your own words, stressing Jesus' teaching on faith.

1. Have the students cut out a picture of a boat from the typing paper.
2. Give each student a piece of blue construction paper with a line drawn across the center. Have the students draw a calm lake on the top half of the paper.
3. Have the students turn the paper upside down and draw a stormy lake on the bottom half of the paper.
4. Color the background (lakes) and the boat. (If you use colored chalk, put fixative over the picture.)
5. With a paper fastener, fasten the boat to the background on the line drawn through the center of the paper. The background can be moved so that the boat will have first a stormy background and then a calm background.

Faith

MUSTARD SEED NECKLACE   Grades 1-8

Materials Needed:

Newspapers
Mustard seeds
Small scrap of wood — 1 per student
White tempera paint
Gold glitter, gold raffia or gold ribbons
Paint brush
Glue
Sandpaper
Small eye screw

You may need aides to help the younger students.

Before Class:

Sand the wood prior to class time for the younger students.

Procedure:

Read the scriptural passage (Luke 17:6) to the students so they understand the symbolism of the mustard seed in relation to faith.

1. Sand the edges of the wood to a smooth finish.
2. Paint the wood with tempera, putting on several coats of paint.
3. Screw an eye screw into the wood.
4. Glue a mustard seed to the center of the wood.
5. Glue gold glitter around the edge of the wood.
6. Insert raffia or ribbon into the eye screw. Tie the ribbon.

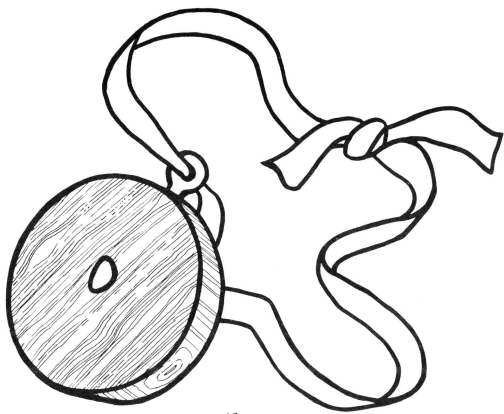

Faith

SEA PAINTING   Grades 1-8

Materials Needed:

12" x 18" white paper
Blue and black tempera paint
Small sponge
Water
Paint brush
Newspapers

Procedure:

Begin this project by reading Matthew 8:23 or by telling the story in your own words, stressing Jesus' teaching on faith.

1. Cover the table with newspapers.
2. Wet the sponge and use blue paint to sponge paint the background blue by dabbing, blotting, or rubbing the paint on white paper. Allow to dry briefly.
3. Use the black paint to paint a boat and voyagers, showing Jesus calming the stormy sea.

CREATION PLACE MATS Grades 1-4

Materials Needed:

Construction paper or 9" x 12" posterboard
"Found" materials from God's creation — dried leaves, dried flowers, weeds, seeds, etc.
Glue or paste
Crayons or felt tip pens
Clear contact paper
Optional: Old magazines, scissors

Procedure:

You may wish to have the students write the words *Thank You, God* at the top of their placemats. Discuss with the students how thankful we should be for all the things God created. When the placemats are used, they can be prayer-starters to thank God for food and all of creation.

1. Arrange "found" materials on the paper. Glue or paste in place.
2. Have each student design his or her name on the placemat, using the crayons or pens.
3. Let the students continue to decorate or design their placemats, using their own imaginations.
4. Seal the finished creation placemats between two pieces of clear contact paper.

   Optional: Have the students cut out magazine pictures which show creation. (trees, flowers, animals, etc.)

Creation

NATURAL NECKLACE   Grades 1-8

Wind yarn around a pine cone or string berries to make a necklace. Make one to keep and one to give away.

Creation

ACROSTIC PRAYER   Grades 1-8

Materials Needed:

White construction paper — 1 per student
Pencils
Crayons or markers

You may need aides to help the younger students with the printing.

Procedure:

1. Have each student print the letters of his or her name vertically on the paper.
2. Have the students think of things in this world for which they would like to thank God. Have the students choose things that begin with each letter in their name. The students should print these things horizontally on their paper, using a letter from their name as the first letter in the word.
3. Have the students embellish their acrostic prayer by illustrating the things for which they are thankful.

CREATION WEAVING   Grades 5-8

Help the students appreciate how wonderfully God has made nature and all living things. In a creation weaving, pull out some of the horizontal threads across the burlap to make an "open weave" area to weave in-and-out some of God's creation in nature.

Materials Needed:

7" x 14" piece of burlap (tan, brown or any earth-tone color)
Variety of weaving material from God's creation (twigs, sticks, dry weeds, dried flowers, leaves, feathers pieces of bark, pods, seeds, rattlesnake skins, corn husks, etc.)
1 heavy stick or piece of wood
Thumb tacks or heavy duty stapler
White glue
Heavy string, cord or yarn

Procedure:

1. Starting three or four inches from the top of the burlap piece:
   Row 1: Pull out about ten rows of threads across the burlap.
   (Note: Always pull the horizontal threads.) Weave a few sticks, weeds, etc. in and out of the up-and-down threads.
   Row 2: Glue on a few leaves or seeds or leave it plain.
   Row 3: Pull out 15 threads and weave in some other material.
2. Continue in the above manner to make a pleasing hanging.
3. At the bottom, pull out threads to make a "fringe."
4. Staple or thumbtack this wall hanging to a large stick or wood.
5. Attach heavy string, cord or yarn to hang on wall.

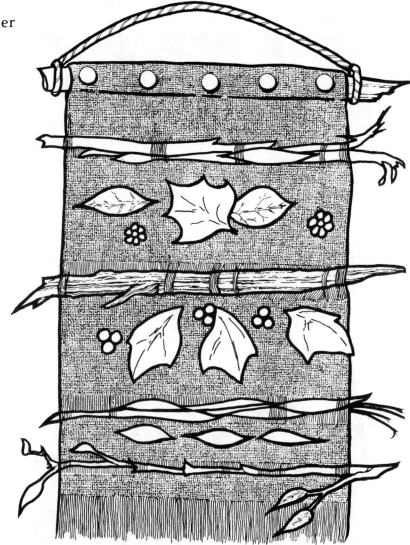

God's Love

ART MURAL   Grades 1-8

This project will work to reinforce the concept of God's love and activity in the lives of the students. Help the students remember that God created the world and all living creatures. Encourage the students to express what this means in their lives.

Materials Needed:

Shelf paper or newsprint
Colored chalk, tempera paint or water colors
Paint brushes
Plastic spray

Procedure:

1. Place the paper either on the floor or attach it to a wall.
2. Have the students express their ideas on paper using chalk, paint or water colors.
3. Allow the students to work in groups on a particular scene.
4. Spray the mural when completed to keep the chalk from rubbing off.
5. Display the mural scenes along the wall.

God's Love

DECOUPAGE WALL PLAQUE   Grades 5-8

Materials Needed:

Wood (appropriate size)
Scissors
File
Dark oak or light walnut stain
Cloth
Candle and matches
Facial tissues
Craft stick
Clear varnish
Small paint brushes
Newspapers, rag and turpentine
Hangers
Glue
Water
Very fine sandpaper or steel wool
Bible verse of student's choice
Felt tip pens
White typing paper
Small container for mixing the glue and water

Before Class:

Use a Bible to find verses about God's love. Choose some passages in advance of this session to offer students ideas and choices such as, "God is love" (1 John 4:8), "Love one another as I have loved you" (John 15:17), "I have called you by name" (Isaiah 49:1), etc. Plan a place to include the name of each student.

Procedure:

1. Using the felt tip pens, have the students neatly letter the verse of their choice on a piece of typing paper smaller than the block of wood.
2. Spread newspapers on the table. Using the scissors, make holes in the wood to imitate wormwood. Make grooves in the wood with the file to make the wood appear worn and beaten. File the edges of the front side of the wood to make it smooth.
3. Using a clean cloth, stain the wood. The best effect is obtained by letting the stain dry for a short time and then wiping off the remaining stain with a facial tissue. Turpentine and a cloth can be used to clean hands.
4. To give an antique effect, slightly burn the edges of the paper with the Bible verse by using a lighted candle. If you do not wish to burn the papers, they may be torn instead.
5. When the stain is dry on the wood, attach the verse to the wood by the following method: Mix ½ tsp. water with ½ tsp. glue. With a craft stick, spread glue over the back of the verse paper. Be sure to cover the entire surface. Place the verse paper in the center of the antiqued wood surface. With a facial tissue, wipe from the center to the edge, making sure all air bubbles are wiped out. Let dry.

6. After the glue is completely dry on the wood, paint both wood and verse paper with clear varnish. After two coats of varnish, sand the wood with very fine sandpaper or steel wool. Varnish several times more, sanding after each coat of varnish. Be sure to let the varnish dry thoroughly before each application.
7. Attach to hangers.

This project can be done in two sessions. Prepare and decorate Bible verse one day. Prepare the wood and complete the plaque another day.

Jesus

MIRROR PICTURE   Grades 1-4

The Apostles were chosen by Jesus to be his friends and to witness to others. God chooses each Christian to do the same in today's world. Today we are going to make a special plaque to hang in your room to remind you that Jesus loves you. Just as the mirror reflects what we look like, Jesus calls us to reflect his love to others.

Materials Needed:

One square (6½" x 6½") of posterboard per student
One small square of mirror (approximately 1½") per student
Felt tip markers
White glue
Yarn or string
Paper punch

Before Class:

Pencil in the letters "Jesus Loves Me" (1" block printing) around the edges of the posterboard. (See drawing for placement of words). You may wish to pre-punch two holes near the top and add the yarn or string to hang.

Procedure:

1. Have the students trace over the letters with felt tip pens.
2. Glue the mirror in the center. Let dry.
3. Punch two holes near the top of the picture and loop a piece of yarn or string to hang.

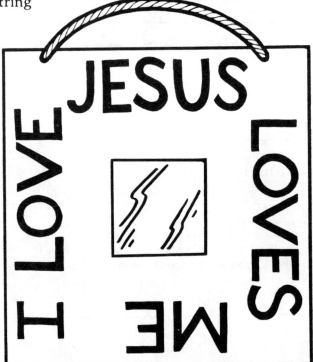

Jesus

VELOUR CHI RHO BOOKMARK   Grades 1-4

The Chi Rho symbol is an ancient monogram of Christ. It appears on altars, bookmarks and vestments. The monogram has been in Christian use for at least 1600 years. The symbol is derived from the first two letters of the Greek XPICTOC (pronounced Christos). The letters abbreviate the name of Christ.

Materials Needed:

Wide velour ribbon or velour paper
Scissors
Pencils
Glue
White felt
Chi Rho pattern

Procedure:

1. Using the pattern, trace and cut a Chi Rho from the velour.
2. Cut out a piece of felt large enough to glue the Chi Rho onto so that there is a border of felt around it (bookmark size).
3. Glue the Chi Rho onto the white felt.

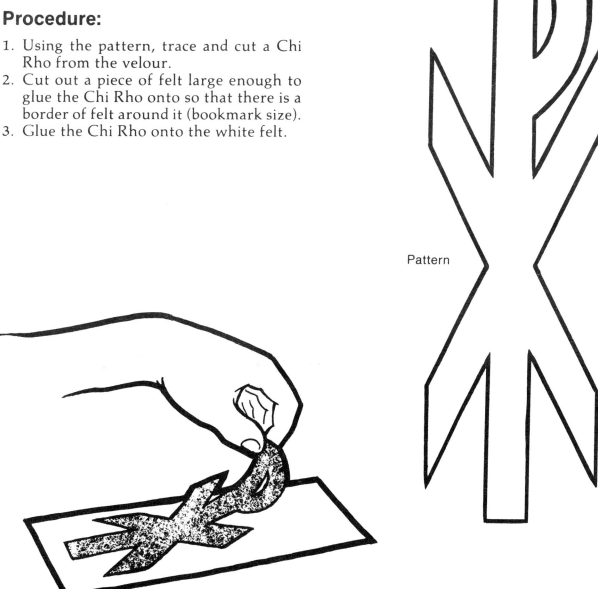

Pattern

YARN ART CREATIONS   Grades 1-4

Materials Needed:

Assorted colors of yarn
Construction paper or velour paper
Glue
Scissors
Crayons
Pencils
Chi Rho pattern (use the pattern in the Mosaic Project)

Procedure:

1. Trace the Chi Rho pattern, an ancient symbol derived from the first two letters of the Greek XPICTOC (meaning Christ) on construction paper. Glue the yarn to the outline of the Chi Rho.
2. Add details with the crayons.
3. If you use velour paper, use a larger piece of contrasting colored construction paper on which to mount the velour.

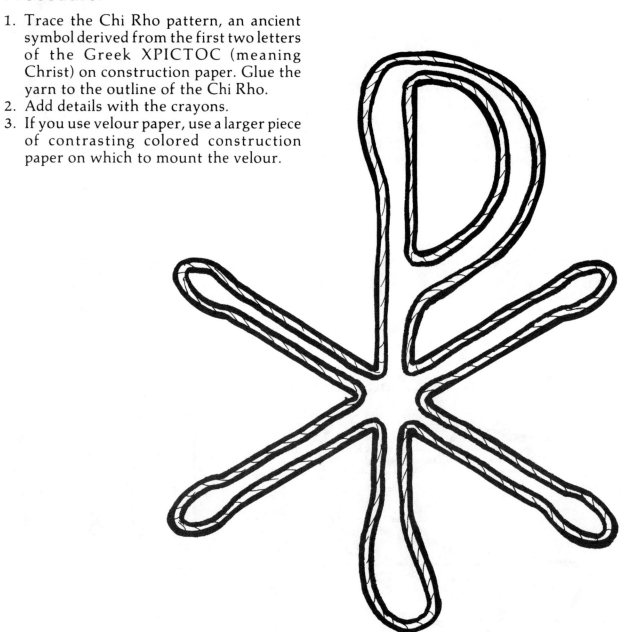

Jesus

BREAD NECKLACE Grades 1-4

Materials Needed:

Small cocktail rye bread
Large alphabet macaroni noodles (#18 size)
White glue
Yarn or ribbon
Acrylic spray fixative

You will need aides for this project.

Before Class:

A few days ahead:
1. Make hole in bread for yarn before bread dries out.
2. Dry bread thoroughly on a cookie sheet in a low temperature oven.
3. Spray both sides of bread with acrylic fixative to preserve.

Procedure:

1. Have the students pick out the alphabet macaroni noodle letters to spell out their name.
2. Glue the letters to the bread. Let dry. Option: Glue name of "Jesus" to other side.
3. Spray bread and noodles with acrylic spray to preserve.
4. Loop yarn or ribbon (approximately 18" long) through the hole in the bread. Tie in a knot.

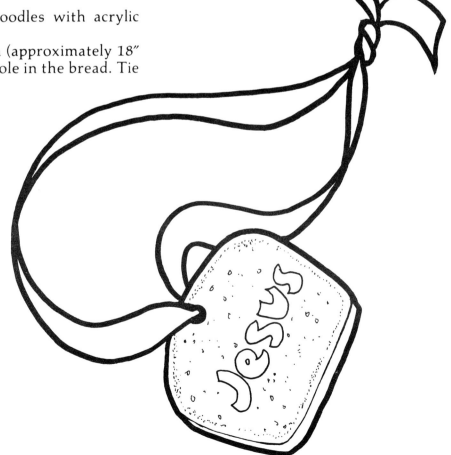

73

Jesus

FISH MOBILE   Grades 1-8

One of the earliest symbols used by Christians to represent Jesus Christ was the fish. It was a secret sign for early believers to identify themselves to each other because they were publicly persecuted for their belief in Jesus. The Greek initials for Jesus Christ, "ICHTHUS" spell out the word *fish* and served as a code to other believers.

Materials Needed:

Green and purple foil
Third contrasting color foil
Cardboard
Wire or thread for mobile
Coat hanger
Glue
Patterns

You will need aides for grades 1 and 2.

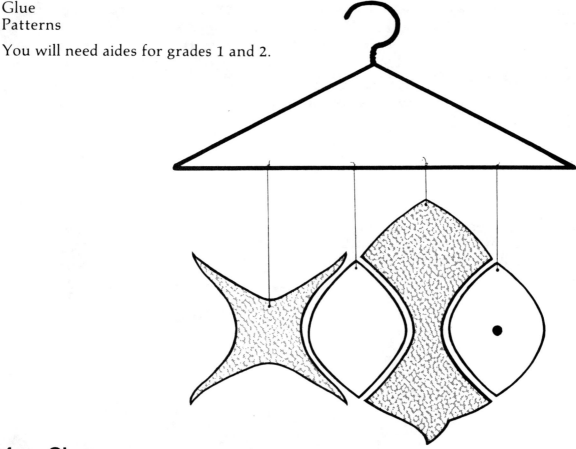

Before Class:

Make up an ample amount of fish segment patterns. For the younger students, trace the segments on the cardboard.

Procedure:

1. Trace the fish segment patterns on a piece of thin cardboard.
2. Cut out each segment individually and cover each piece with green foil. Use contrasting colored foil for the other side of the segments.
3. Cut out scales in purple foil and glue onto the green foil.
4. Attach each segment to a length of thread or wire. Attach all four fish segments to a coat hanger for hanging.

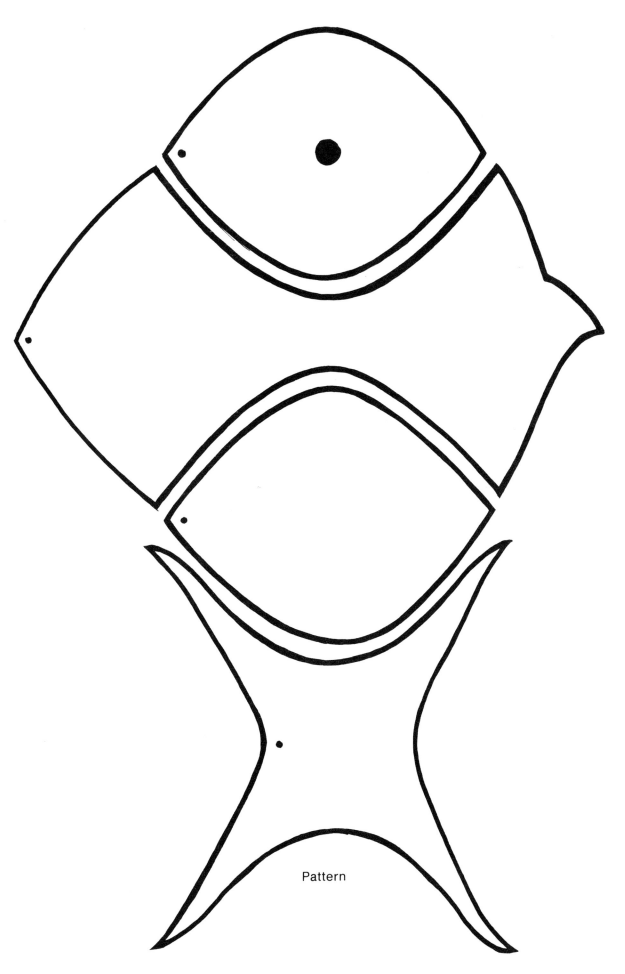

Pattern

Jesus

CLAY FIGURINE   Grades 1-8

Have the students make a figurine from crazy clay. They should think of how Jesus lived. Consider the following:

1. The birth of Jesus
2. Jesus teaching the elders in the temple
3. Jesus with the fishermen
4. Jesus praying on the mountain
5. Jesus calming the sea from a boat
6. Jesus breaking bread with friends
7. Jesus crucified
8. The resurrection of Jesus
9. Any appropriate symbol

Materials Needed:

Wooden spoon
Bowl
Paint brush
Paints
Clear nail polish
Plastic bag
Newspapers

Crazy Clay Recipe:
1 cup flour
¼ cup salt
1/3 cup water

You will need aides for the younger students.

Before Class:

For the younger students, make the crazy clay ahead of time.

Procedure:

1. Pour flour, salt and water in a bowl. Mix. If the clay feels dry, add a few drops of water. If it's too mushy, add flour. (Use clay at room temperature. The clay may be stored in a plastic bag in the refrigerator until ready to use.)
2. Use the clay to make a figurine of Jesus which depicts a part of his life.
3. After the figurine is made, paint it with a waterbase paint. Give it a glossy look with a coat of clear nail polish.

Jesus

WOOD BLOCK   Grades 1-8

Materials Needed:

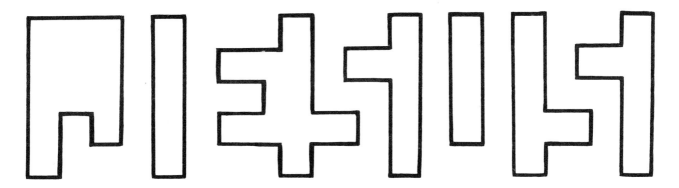

1 pattern for each student
Carbon paper
Pencils
Block of wood cut 5½" x 8½"
Black fine-point felt tip pen (permanent)
Rulers
Sandpaper
Masking tape

Before Class:

Have the pattern traced onto wood for students in grades 1 and 2. You can do this project on posterboard, if you prefer.

Procedure:

1. Sand wood, if necessary.
2. Place carbon paper between wood and pattern.
3. Carefully trace pattern onto wood (You may wish to use masking tape to hold pattern to wood.)
4. Remove pattern and carbon paper carefully.
5. Trace over the carbon lines with felt tip pen. Use a ruler if necessary.
6. Older students can "wood burn" the design if you can get sufficient wood burning sets. Have the pattern traced onto wood for your students in grades 1 and 2. You can do this project on posterboard, if you prefer.
7. Discover the name you have made from the pattern is Jesus. Through all our liturgical seasons and everyday, we are to follow Jesus.

Pattern

JESUS POEM/QUOTATION PLAQUE   Grades 1-8

Materials Needed:

Copies of a suitable poem, quotation or Bible verse about Jesus
Wood (5" x 6") — 1 per student
Glue
Sandpaper
Hangers
Varnish or acrylic polymer
Brush
Newspaper
Optional: Clear contact paper

Procedure:

1. Attach a hanger to the back of the plaque. (Metal pop top tabs make excellent hangers. Use a small nail or tack to attach the hanger to back of plaque.)
2. Sand the wood, if necessary.
3. Glue quotation, verse or poem to the center of the wood. Let dry.
4. Apply a thin coat of varnish or polymer over the top to protect the surface. If you wish to cover the quotation with a piece of clear contact paper, you do not need to varnish. (You may wish to paint the wood instead of varnishing it.)

"I am the good
    shepherd;
I know my own
    and my own know me . . ."

—John 10:14

Sample Quotation Card

Jesus

CERAMIC TILE WALL PLAQUE   Grades 5-8

Materials Needed:

Copies of a suitable poem, quotation or Bible verse about Jesus
Wood (5" x 6") — 1 per student
Glue
Sandpaper
Hangers
Varnish or acrylic polymer
Brush
Newspaper
1" ceramic tiles — 18 per student
Rickrack or ribbon for decoration around plaque

Procedure:

1. Arrange the ceramic tiles around the edge of the wood. Glue the tiles down.
2. Glue the quotation in the center.
3. Glue rickrack, ribbon or any suitable decoration around the edge of quotation.
4. Add the hanger.

"I am the good
shepherd;
I know my own
and my own know me . . ."

—John 10:14

CRAYON-ON-CHALK TRANSFER ETCHING
Grades 1-8

Materials Needed:

Newspapers
Two sheets of manilla or white drawing paper identical in size for each student
Yellow chalk
Dark crayon
Sharp pencil
INRI pattern
Optional: Crayons or paints
     and brushes, scissors

Procedure:

1. Cover one of the sheets of paper with a heavy coat of yellow chalk.
2. Heavily apply a layer of dark crayon so the chalk is completey covered.
3. Lay the clean sheet of paper over the sheet covered with crayon. Using your sharp pencil, trace the pattern upon the uncolored sheet. Press hard, working on a hard surface so that the transfer etching will be clear. You may shade the inside of the letters or design the letters in various ways.
4. When you remove the top sheet, you will find that the pencil drawing has caused the crayon wax to leave the chalk backing.
5. The initials INRI represent the title, "Jesus of Nazareth, King of the Jews." (John 19:19) Other designs can be used.
6. Optional: For younger children, use the block letters INRI or other design and copy one for each student. Let them color or paint the letters. They could also cut out each letter and paste it on a darker sheet of construction paper.

Jesus

BIBLE STORY DIORAMA   Grades 3-8

Materials Needed:

Shoebox
Scraps of fabric
Colored paper
Clay or playdough
Cardboard
Glue and tape
Scissors
Pencils

Procedure:

1. Have a group of students work on a project together or they may work individually. Have the students decide which scene about Jesus' life they are going to portray.
2. Decorate the inside of the shoebox with scraps of fabric or paper.
3. Using clay, shape the characters in the story. Place the figures in the shoebox.

MOSAIC Grades 3-8

Materials Needed:

Patterns
Black yarn
Aquarium gravel — various colors
Epoxy cement
Firm cardboard, size 5" x 7"
White glue

Procedure:

1. Trace one of the patterns onto the cardboard or design your own. Using white glue, outline the pattern with the black yarn.
2. Fill in the pattern using various colors of aquarium gravel. Set the gravel by using epoxy cement.
3. Let the mosaic dry 24 hours before taking it home.

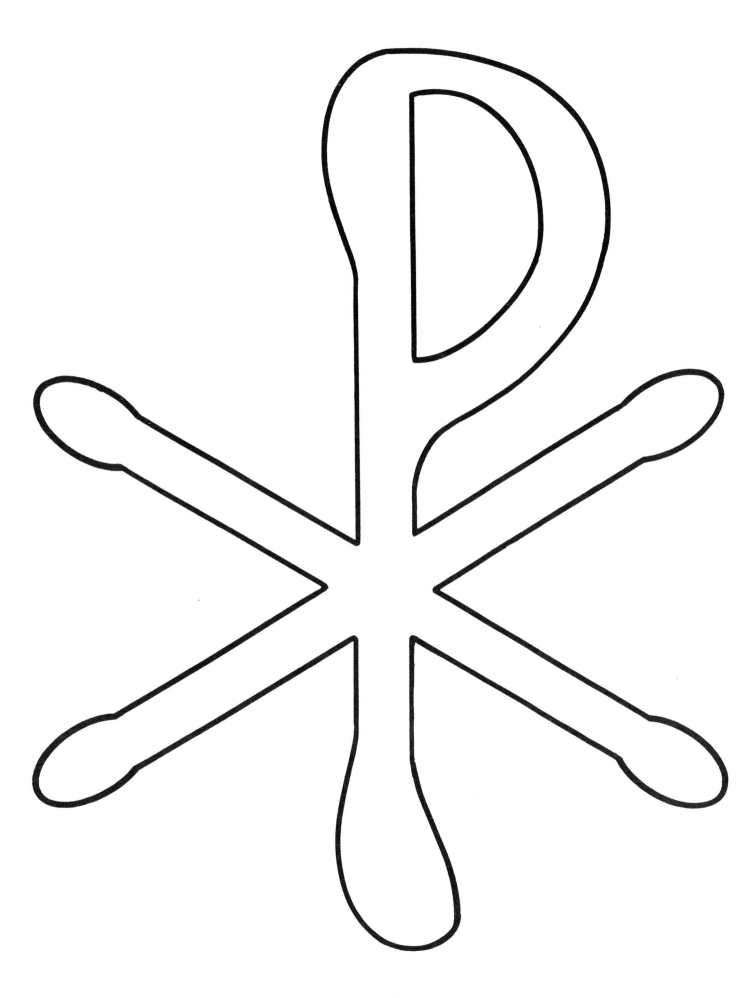

Jesus

BREAD OF LIFE MAGNET   Grades 5-8

Materials Needed:

Small cocktail rye bread
Large alphabet macaroni noodles (#18 size)
Ribbon, needle and thread to sew bow
Roll of burlap strips (1½" wide)
Magnetic strip tape
White glue ("Sobo" glue works well)
Tiny dried flowers
Acrylic spray fixative
Optional: Toothpicks

Before Class:

A few days before:
1. Dry bread thoroughly. Leave out or place in oven at low temperature.
2. Spray both sides of dried bread with an acrylic spray fixative to preserve.
3. Cut burlap strips into 8" pieces.

Procedure:

1. In the middle of the burlap strip, glue two or three flowers.
2. Glue bread over stems of flowers, carefully pressing burlap to back of bread. Glue well.
3. Arrange letters on the bread. Glue to the bread. Toothpicks may be helpful to place letters. Suggested wording: "I am the Bread of Life." "Give us this day our daily bread." "Bread broken, bread shared."
4. When glue is dry, spray bread and noodles with acrylic spray.
5. Glue or sew ribbon to the top of the burlap.
6. Attach two small pieces of magnetic tape to the back of the burlap behind the bow.

Jesus

TELE-VIEWER   Grades 5-8

Materials Needed:

Square cardboard box or carton — 1 per student
White window shade 9" wide or a roll of white shelving paper — 1 per student
Water color paints or crayons
Scissors
Ruler
Pencil
Knife
Cardboard tube from paper towels — 2 per student
Tape

Procedure:

1. Remove the front section of the box and discard.
2. Draw a line 1" in on each side and 1" from bottom.
3. Cut along this line to make "slots" for the paper to slide through.
4. On the entire window shade or roll of paper, paint a story scene about any part of the life of Christ, allowing each picture to be "framed" in the center section of the box.
5. Tape or glue the ends of the window shade or roll of paper to the cardboard tube.
6. Insert the story scene and unroll the pictures as the story proceeds.
7. As the story proceeds, have each student take a turn narrating what is happening in each frame of the story.

You may suggest the events of the Christmas story, Jesus' ministry or his death and Resurrection. Brainstorm Bible stories that the students particularly like. If the Christmas story is used, play or sing a familiar Christmas carol as background music while doing this project.

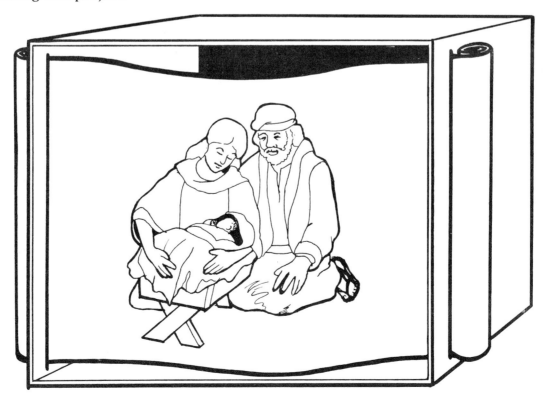

Jesus (Christmas)

CHRISTMAS PAPER WEIGHT   Grades 1-8

Materials Needed:

Per Student:

Baby food jar or jam jar with screw cap
One piece white styrofoam (3" square)
Small wad of floral clay
Several small pine branches
Miniature toy novelties depicting Christmas
Paste brush
Water
Transparent glue
Small piece of blue felt (3" square)
Two tablespoons moth flakes
Scissors

You will need a number of aides to help pre-cut everything for students in grades 1 and 2 and to help them assemble the project.

Procedure:

1. Using the jar lid as pattern, cut out a round piece of styrofoam.
2. Cover the inside of the screw cap with a thin layer of clay.
3. Press the styrofoam firmly on top of the clay.
4. With pine branches and small toy novelties, build a Christmas scene on the styrofoam. (A small piece of floral clay under the branches and toy novelties will secure them firmly in position.)
5. Fill the jar with water. Add the mothflakes.
6. With a paste brush, dab thin layer of glue on the opening of the jar and on the rim of the screw cap.
7. Screw the lid on the jar tightly. Let dry overnight before inverting jar.
8. Cut and paste blue felt to fit bottom of cap.

Holy Spirit

HOLY SPIRIT NECKLACE   Grades 1-8

Say the prayer, "Come Holy Spirit, fill the hearts of the faithful and renew the face of the earth." Remind the students to wear the necklace they will be making as a sign to others that they share God's life-giving Spirit. As they care for others, they will be renewing the face of the earth.

Materials Needed:

Wooden dove (with hole drilled) — 1 per student
Twine
Acrylic or tempera paint
Small brushes
Paint shirt
Newspapers
Felt tip pens, markers and/or crayons

Before Class:

For the younger students, print the words "Renew the face of the earth" on the dove.

Procedure:

1. Cover the tables with newspapers. Have the students wear paint shirts.
2. Have the students write the words "Renew the face of the earth" very carefully on the dove.
3. Let the students paint and decorate their doves. Felt tip pens or crayons may also be used, depending on the type of wood that is used.
4. Push the twine through the hole and make a knot. Use a length of twine 18" to 20" as the "chain" for the necklace.

FRUIT OF THE SPIRIT TREE   Grades 1-8

Read Galatians 5:22 from the Bible. This project can be used to help students get in touch with the Holy Spirit as a special power in the life of each person who is following the example of Jesus. Use straws to "paint" a tree. Help the students understand the concept of the Holy Spirit by showing them that when they blow through the straw, they cannot really see their breath, but can see the results as their breath moves the paint. The power of the Holy Spirit is a lot like their unseen breath that has the power to move the paint on the paper. We cannot see the Holy Spirit but we can experience the results of what happens when we cooperate with the love of God.

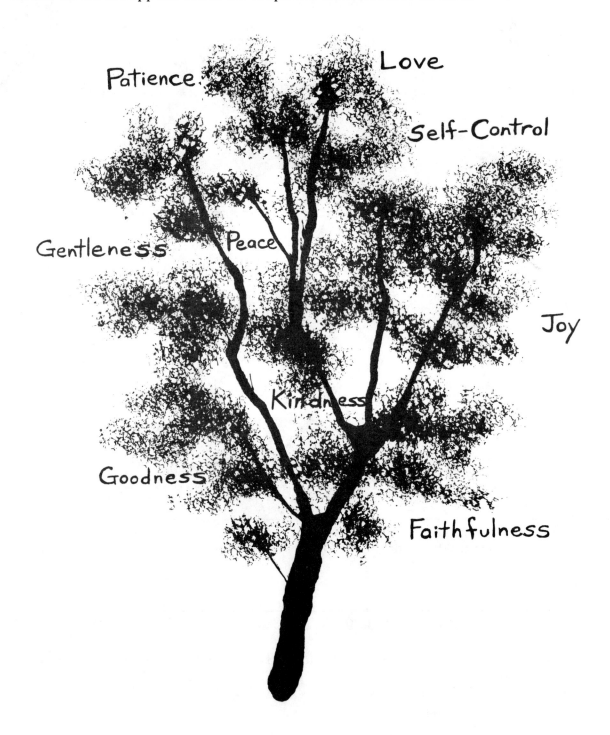

Materials Needed:

Construction or rice paper (12" x 16")
Black tempera paint for tree trunk
Green, yellow, orange tempera paint for leaves
Straws
Paint shirts or old clothes
Small piece of sponge
Clip-type clothespins
Newspapers
Tissue or crepe paper in various colors
Old magazines
Black felt tip pens
Water
Container for mixing paint and water
Crayons
Pencils
Optional: Small paint brushes

Before Class:

Write the verse from Galatians 5:22 on the board. Underline the fruit or list the fruits the Holy Spirit wishes to produce in us. You may wish to make up fruit shapes with the words printed on them for grades 1 and 2. Students may glue or paste the fruit to the tree.

Procedure:

1. Cover tables well with newspapers.
2. Thin down black tempera paint (½ paint and ½ water).
3. Drop a blob of this black paint on bottom half of paper.
4. Blow through the straw to "move" the paint to make a tree. Keep blowing to make more branches.
5. To make leaves, pinch a piece of sponge with a clothespin. Using the clothespin as a handle, dip the sponge into the green, yellow or orange tempera paint and "sponge" on leaves.
   Some other ideas for leaves are: a) Using a small paint brush and tempera paint, dot and/or "swirl" the brush on the paper; b) Twist little pieces of tissue or crepe paper and glue or paste to branches; c) Cut out leaves of fruit or flowers from magazines and glue or paste to branches; d) Cut out pictures from magazines that show examples of people doing good things that symbolize the "fruit of the Spirit" and paste onto branches. Examples are: Love — mother and child, family hugging, etc.; Joy — balloons, smiling and laughing faces, etc.; Peace — sunset, lake, tiny animal asleep, etc.
6. Let dry.
7. Add "fruit" to the tree by writing the following words at the top of the branches or among the leaves: Love, Joy, Peace, Patience, Kindness, Goodness, Faithfulness, Gentleness, Self-Control. Use a pencil, black felt tip pen, crayons, etc. to write the words.
8. Mount on another piece of construction paper to make a frame. Title your painting "Fruit of the Spirit" Tree.

Holy Spirit

SUNCATCHERS   Grades 1-8

The Holy Spirit is God's presence within us. "A new heart I will give you and a new Spirit I will put within you." (Ezekiel 36:26-27) Our attitude and actions are shaped by the loving presence of the Holy Spirit which is God's life within us.

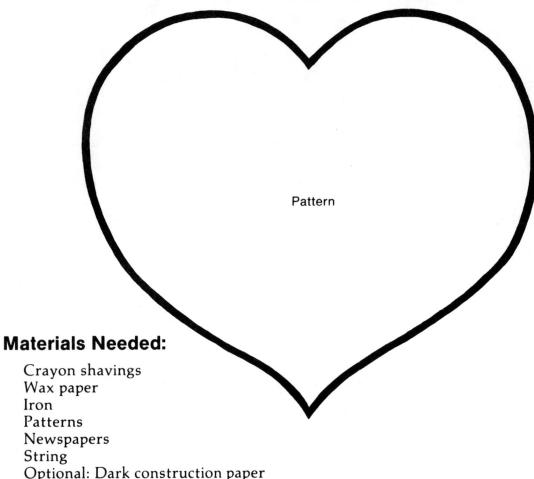

Pattern

Materials Needed:

Crayon shavings
Wax paper
Iron
Patterns
Newspapers
String
Optional: Dark construction paper

You will want to use aides with the younger students.

Before Class:

Prepare patterns and make samples for the students to see.

Procedure:

1. Spread newspapers over working surface.
2. Place a pattern on the newspaper as a guide.
3. Lay a piece of clear kitchen wax paper on top of the newspaper according to the size desired.
4. Drop shavings of crayons onto the wax paper with the pattern as a guide.
5. Lay another piece of wax paper on top of the crayon shavings.
6. Place the sandwiched sheets between layers of newspaper and press with a warm iron for a stained-glass effect. Adults only should do the ironing.
7. Mat with dark construction paper or display in a window by cutting around the symbol and attaching a string for hanging.

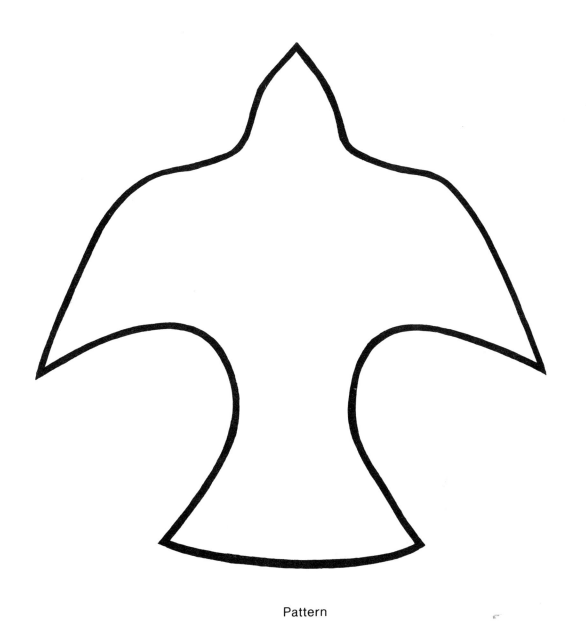

Pattern

Apostles

CRAYON ETCHING   Grades 1-8

Materials Needed:

White paper
Crayons
India ink or black crayon
Pen for etching

Procedure:

1. Use several different bright colors of crayons to completely cover the white paper any way desired.
2. Brush the paper with india ink or color over the paper with black crayon.
3. When ink is dry, use a pen to etch a picture on the paper. One idea is to etch a picture of the Holy Spirit descending upon the apostles on Pentecost.
4. At the bottom of the etching, the older students can list the names of the apostles.

Resurrection

POTTED PLANTS   Grades 1-4

Materials Needed:

Small paper cup — 1 per student
Vegetable or flower seeds of any variety
Potting soil
Newspaper
Rags for cleanup
Water

Procedure:

1. Have the students use the newspapers to cover their work surface.
2. Give a paper cup and seeds to each student.
3. Pass out the potting soil and have the students plant the seeds.
4. Water the soil slightly and have the students care for the seeds at home by putting the potted seeds on a window sill and watering them regularly.

Resurrection

WATER TUMBLER VEGETABLE GARDEN   Grades 1-4

Materials Needed:

Water tumbler — 1 per student (use old jars such as jelly or peanut butter jars)
Four toothpicks for each student
One large sweet potato or large carrot per student
Water

In advance of this session, send a note home asking the parents to send a vegetable for this session.

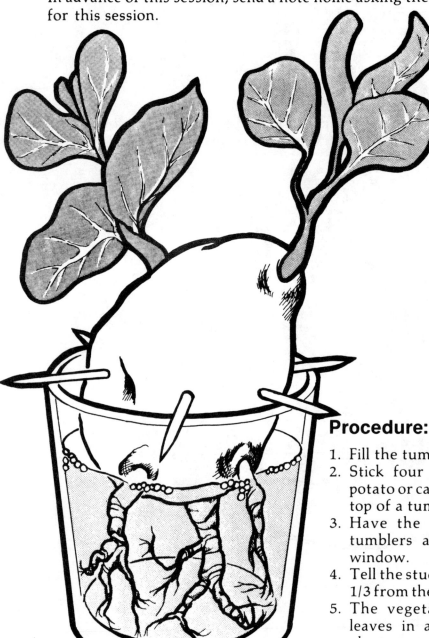

Procedure:

1. Fill the tumblers 2/3 full of water.
2. Stick four or more toothpicks into a potato or carrot and balance them on the top of a tumbler.
3. Have the students take home their tumblers and keep them in a sunny window.
4. Tell the students to refill the tumblers to 1/3 from the top as the water evaporates.
5. The vegetables will grow roots and leaves in about six weeks. Then the plants may be planted in soil.

Note: Send directions for this project home with the students. You could have the students wait to fill the tumblers with water until they get home.

Resurrection

BUTTERFLY Grades 1-4

Materials Needed:

Colored tissue or crepe paper
6" chenille wire or pipe cleaner
Glue
Glitter
Pattern

Procedure:

1. Using the pattern provided, cut butterfly wings on the fold line from a 4½" square of folded paper.
2. Decorate the wings and apply glue. Shake on glitter.
3. Bend the chenille wire in half, slip wings between wire, and gather the colored paper somewhat between the wire.
4. Twist the ends of the wire to make antennae for the butterfly.

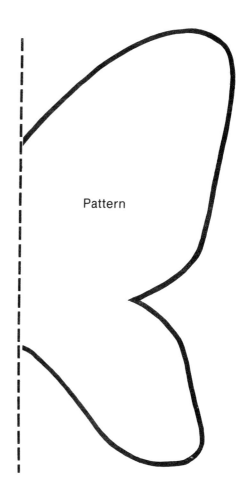

Pattern

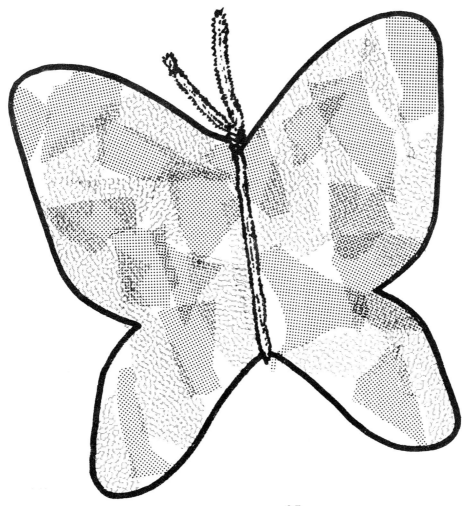

GARDEN TERRARIUM   Grades 1-8

Materials Needed:

Vegetable, flower or tree seeds
Potting soil
Bottle or jar with a large mouth
Spoon
Popsicle stick
Small artificial flowers
Pebbles or small plastic animal figurines
Water

Procedure:

1. Thoroughly clean the jar and remove all labels.
2. Lay the jar on its side. Put loose soil in the jar by using a spoon.
3. Using a flat stick, plant seeds below the soil.
4. Carefully add the artificial flowers, pebbles or little animal figurines.
5. Using a spoon, water the planted seeds and then place the jar in the sun. Be sure to water the seeds daily.

Resurrection

RESURRECTION SHADOW PICTURE   Grades 1-8

Materials Needed:

9-inch aluminum pie pan — 1 per student
Black felt
Black rickrack
Glue
Scissors
Hanger
Pattern

You will need aides for grades 1 and 2.

Procedure:

1. Using the pattern provided, cut out a silhouette of the risen Christ from black felt.
   Cut out several clouds from black felt.
2. Glue the silhouette of Christ and the clouds on the inside of the pie pan.
3. Glue rickrack around the edge of the pan to make a frame.
4. Glue a hanger on the back. The hanger can be purchased or made from cardboard
   with a hole punched in one end.

TISSUE BUTTERFLIES   Grades 5-8

Materials Needed:

Newspaper
Wax paper
Colored tissue paper in different colors
Thin pliable wire
Chenille wire or pipe cleaner
Cardboard
White glue
Small container for mixing glue and water
Brushes
Water
String
Acrylic polymer
Pattern

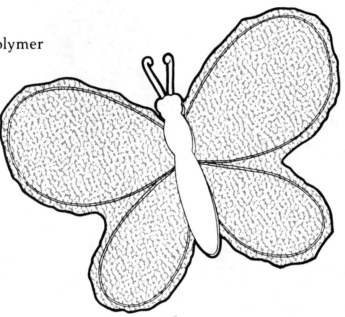

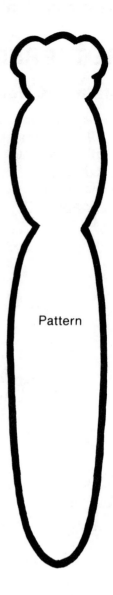

Pattern

Procedure:

1. Using the pattern, cut two body pieces for the butterfly from the cardboard (head, body and tail piece).
2. Shape wire for both the large and small wings, keeping both sides of each wing the same size.
3. Place newspaper on the table. Cover the newspaper with a large sheet of wax paper. Place tissue on the wax paper and place the wire wing on the tissue.
4. Brush white glue about an inch wide on and over the wire. Glue may be thinned with water. Place another tissue over the wire, press tissue paper together and let dry. Trim off the excess paper.
5. Interesting shapes may be designed on the wings using contrasting colors of tissue paper.
6. Glue the ends of the wings between the two pieces of cardboard body. Then glue chenille wire between the cardboard pieces to make feelers.
7. When decorating the head, body and tail piece of the butterfly, repeat the tissue colors of the wings.
8. After the butterfly is dry, paint it with acrylic polymer. Acrylic polymer may be thinned with water. Use equal amounts of polymer and water.
9. Add string to hang the butterfly.

BUTTERFLY MOBILE   Grades 5-8

Materials Needed:

Wax paper
Colored tissue paper
Thread
Small stick or dowel rod
Iron
Scissors

Procedure:

1. Tear off two pieces of wax paper about a foot long.
2. On one piece of wax paper, arrange scraps of colored tissue paper in shapes to look like butterflies.
3. Place the other piece of wax paper over these shapes and gently press with a warm iron to seal the design between the wax papers.
4. Cut out the butterflies, leaving about ¼" edge around each butterfly design. Tie them with thread to a small stick or dowel, hanging them at different lengths.

Resurrection (Lent)

FROM COCOONS TO BUTTERFLIES   Grades 5-8

Discuss Lent with the students. Explain that it is a time to re-examine our lives with the purpose of growing more like Jesus. Using the caterpillar into butterfly cycle, talk about how Jesus died out of love for us and how God raised Jesus up again to new life. Explain how we celebrate this belief at Easter when there is new life all around us.

PART I (This is a 2-part project)

Materials Needed:

    2" wide slips of note paper
    Newsprint in strips
    Paste/water mixture or flour/water mixture
    Tray
    Water
    Sponge
    Paper towels
    Pencil or pen

Procedure:

Direct the students to write a letter to Jesus, telling him what they plan to do during Lent to change themselves into better persons. Use small slips of paper, about 2" wide. Suggest positive actions of helping others, etc. Roll up the finished letters. Strips of newsprint, dipped in a paste/water mixture or a flour/water mixture, are then rolled around each letter. Several strips are needed for each letter. The little "cocoons" may then be placed on a cookie tray to dry. A slip of paper on which the student's name is written may be placed under his or her cocoon for later identification. The cocoons will dry in a few days into hard shells.

Clean hands and work areas with water, sponge and paper towels.

PART II

Review:

Talk about how the students made cocoons in which the students placed a note to Jesus stating what they would do during Lent to help change themselves into better persons to grow as more loving persons. The caterpillar in the cocoon is transformed into a beautiful butterfly, into a new kind of life.

Discuss the fact that when Jesus died and was buried, he also changed into a new kind of life with God. We say that he rose from the dead.

Tell the students that perhaps in this past month they changed a small part of themselves as they tried to be loving to others. If they failed, they can try again. Ask the students to keep the butterfly as a reminder of this challenge.

Materials Needed:

White construction paper
Crayons
Butterfly pattern
Scissors
Pins
Pipe cleaner

Procedure:

1. Trace the butterfly pattern onto white construction paper.
2. Color and cut out the butterflies.
3. Color the body of the cocoon.
4. Attach the cocoon to the body with pins.
5. Twist a pipe cleaner around the body, just under the head. Twist to make antennae.

(Put the student's name on the back of his or her butterfly if the butterflies are to be distributed later.)

Pattern

Prayer

CENTERPIECE CANDLE   Grades 5-8

Materials Needed:

Tree bark
New or used candles
Pen knife
Plasticine
Straw flowers
Sewing needles
Glass head pins
Tweezers

Option One:

A piece of bark makes a fine holder for a plain candle. Scoop out a hollow with a pen knife, line it with plasticine, and push the candle in firmly. Decorate with straw flowers pushed tightly against the candle and secure with glass head pins.

Option Two:

Use a plain candle, either a pillar candle or a short wide one. Pierce a pattern of holes in the candle with a fine sewing needle. Press a star flower head into each hole using tweezers to handle the flowers. The candles can sit in a plain saucer.

Prayer

SAY IT WITH TAMBOURINES   Grades 1-4

Read Psalm 150:1-6, "We will make our own musical instruments to praise the Lord."

Materials Needed:

Paper plates
Paper punch
Bells
Yarn
Crayons or felt tip markers

Procedure:

1. Hold the faces of two paper plates together and punch holes around the edges.
2. Use a piece of yarn to tie a bell at each hole.
3. Use crayons or markers to decorate.
4. Pray Psalm 150 together and make a joyful noise with the tambourines.

Prayer

RHYTHM MARACAS   Grades 1-4

Materials Needed:

Salt carton
Beans
Tape
Constrution paper
Dowel rod
Optional: Yarn for decorating

Procedure:

1. Put a few beans in an empty salt carton. Tape the carton shut.
2. Cover the carton with construction paper.
3. For the handle, make a hole in the top and bottom of the carton and push a dowel rod through the carton. Optional: Tie pieces of yarn on one end of the dowel rod.
4. Sing a happy song about God's goodness and play the maracas to accompany the singing.

Prayer

ANGELUS FELT PICTURE   Grades 1-8

Materials Needed:

Felt material for background
Various colors of felt material for the patterns
Picture frame
Glue
Cardboard
Pencils
Scissors
Patterns

Before Class:

Pre-cut picture pieces and felt pieces for the younger students.

Procedure:

1. For each picture piece, trace a pattern on the felt, using the pattern provided.
2. Fit picture to frame size to be used.
3. Cut colored felt into pieces. Use gold for halo, blue for gown, etc.
4. Glue to felt material background and insert into frame as a picture.

Flowers

Halos

Stems

Angel Body

Angel Hair

Hands

Mary Body

Sun

Faces

Wing

Wing

Pattern

107

Prayer

PRAYER OF ST. FRANCIS WOOD-BURN Grades 3-8

Materials Needed:

Magazines for pictures of birds and animals
Copies of the *Prayer of St. Francis* — 1 per student
Scissors
Newspaper
Wood — 1 per student
Craft stick
Hangers
Clear stain
Glue
Cloth for staining
Water
Container for mixing glue and water
Clear varnish
Paintbrush
Steel wool or sandpaper
Facial tissue
Matches
Candle

This project requires two sessions.

Procedure:

1. Cut out pictures of birds and animals from the magazines.
2. Using the following instructions, decoupage the pictures and the prayer.
   a. Spread newspapers on a table.
   b. Stain the wood, using a cloth. The best effect is obtained by letting the stain dry for a short time and then wiping off the remaining stain with a facial tissue.
   c. Burn the edges of the pictures using a lighted candle to give an antique effect. If you do not wish to burn the pictures, they may be torn instead.
   d. When the stain is dry on the wood, adhere the pictures to the wood by the following method: Mix ½ tsp. water with ½ tsp. glue. With a craft stick, spread the glue over the back of the picture. Be sure to cover the entire surface. Place the pictures and the copy of the prayer in an attractive manner. Wipe from the center to the edge of the picture with a facial tissue, making sure all the air bubbles are wiped out. Let dry.
   e. After the glue is completely dry on the wood, paint both the wood and pictures with clear varnish. After two coats of varnish, sand with very fine steel wool. Varnish thoroughly before each application.
3. Attach to hangers.

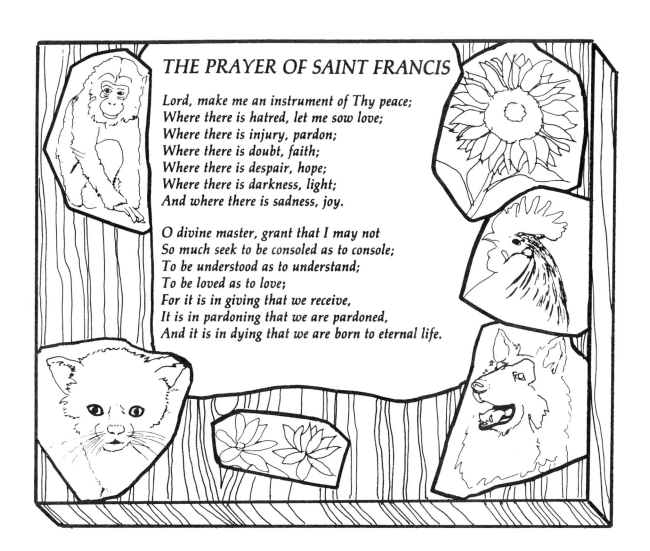

THE PRAYER OF SAINT FRANCIS

Lord, make me an instrument of Thy peace;
Where there is hatred, let me sow love;
Where there is injury, pardon;
Where there is doubt, faith;
Where there is despair, hope;
Where there is darkness, light;
And where there is sadness, joy.

O divine master, grant that I may not
So much seek to be consoled as to console;
To be understood as to understand;
To be loved as to love;
For it is in giving that we receive,
It is in pardoning that we are pardoned,
And it is in dying that we are born to eternal life.

Prayer

STARBURST CROSS   Grades 5-8

Materials Needed:

Toothpicks (round)
White glue
Brushes
Cardboard
Gold spray paint
Pencils
Scissors

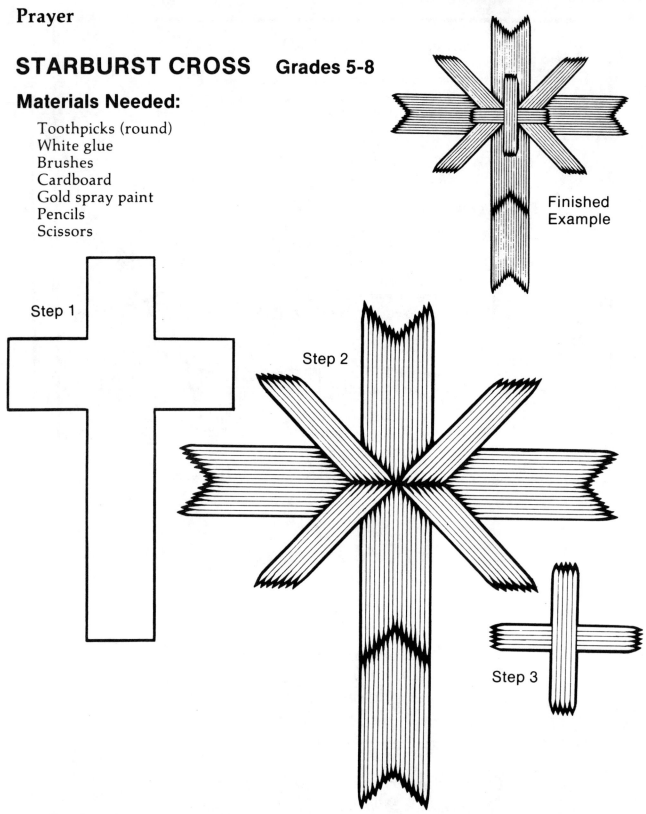

Finished
Example

Step 1

Step 2

Step 3

Procedure:

1. On cardboard, draw a cross about 7" long with 1¼" wide cross bars. Cut out the cross.
2. Brush on a coat of glue and place toothpicks as shown in the drawing.
3. Glue toothpicks to arms.
4. Add another "cross" of toothpicks over the first one.
5. When dry, spray with gold paint.

110

LITURGICAL CALENDAR   Grades 1-8

Materials Needed:

Colored pencils or crayons
Copies of the liturgical calendar
Magazines
Old Christmas and Easter cards
Scissors
Glue

Before Class:

Prepare ample patterns for younger students.

Procedure:

1. Pass out copies of the liturgical calendar.
2. Have the students draw the symbols for each season on their liturgical calendar. (You may wish to list the seasons and their symbols on a chalkboard and provide patterns for the younger students.)
3. Older students should be able to determine for themselves what symbol applies to each liturgical season. Students may draw liturgical symbols on the appropriate season.
4. Students may cut out pictures from magazines, old Christmas cards and Easter cards to paste on their liturgical calendar.

111

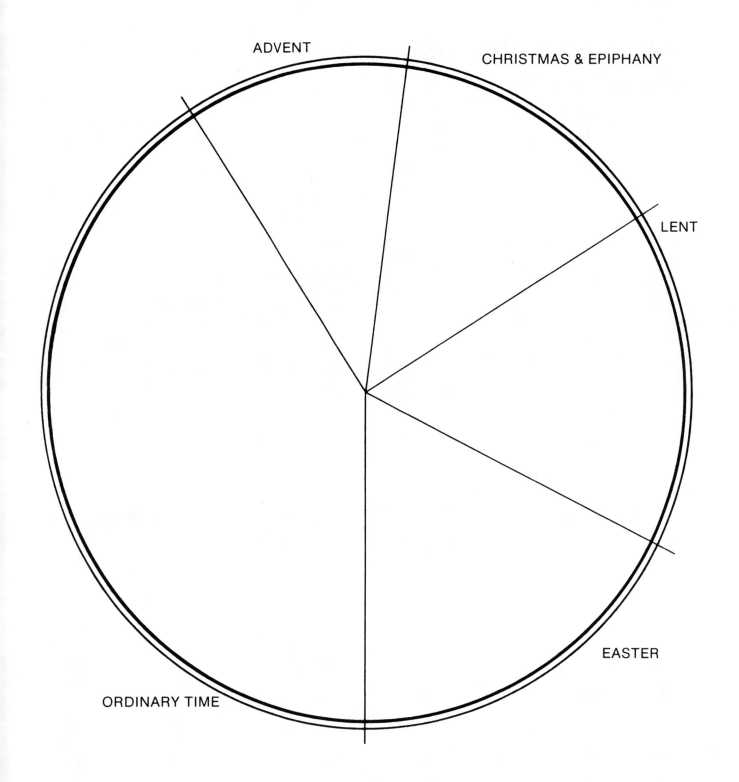

ADVENT

CHRISTMAS & EPIPHANY

LENT

EASTER

ORDINARY TIME

ADVENT: Advent Wreath, Candle
CHRISTMAS: Star, Nativity Scene, Manger, Gift Box
LENT: Cross, Crown of Thorns, Palms
EASTER: Lily, Candle, Plant, Butterfly, Lamb
ORDINARY TIME: Tree, Vine and Branches

Rosary

ROSARY POSTER   Grades 1-4

October 7th is the feast day of Our Lady of the Rosary. A rosary is a set of beads (or knots) to help people pray the *Our Father* and *Hail Mary* prayers in five decades while remembering the events in the life of Jesus and Mary. The months of October and May are the two months especially devoted to Mary.

Materials Needed:

Large posterboard
Round "confetti" (use paper punch on construction paper)
Glue
Crayons
Pencil
Diagram of rosary
Optional: Cheerios

Before Class:

Make up bags of confetti. Pencil in the rosary on the posterboard for grades 1 and 2. Make an "x" or "o" where students are to glue dots (beads).

Procedure:

1. Lightly pencil in a drawing of a rosary.
2. Glue confetti (or Cheerios) in appropriate places.
3. Draw a cross with the crayons.

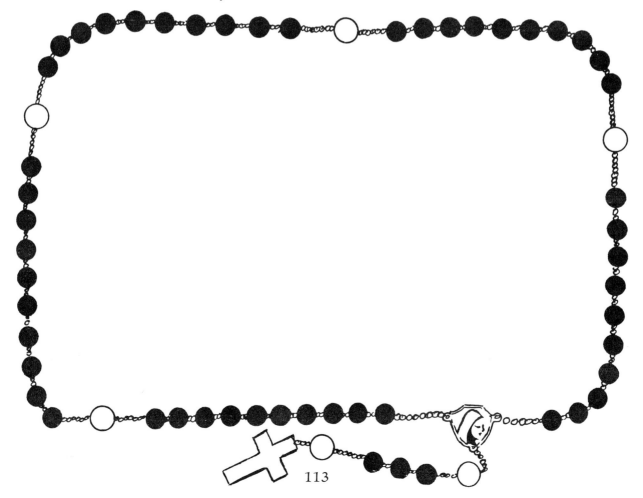

113

BAKER'S CLAY ROSARY   Grades 3-8

This rosary project takes two sessions.

See recipe for "Baker's Clay" under "Baker's Clay Magnets" project.

Materials Needed:

"Baker's Clay" recipe
Large needlepoint needles
Clear nail polish
Heavy string

First Session: Make beads and cross out of "Baker's Clay." Roll dough into small balls to make beads according to desired size. Make "Hail Mary" beads smaller than "Our Father" beads. Five decades of the rosary require a total of 53 small beads and 6 larger beads. Make holes in beads and in the top of cross with large needlepoint needle before baking. Bake.

Second Session: String beads to make Rosary. Beads may be painted with clear nail polish.

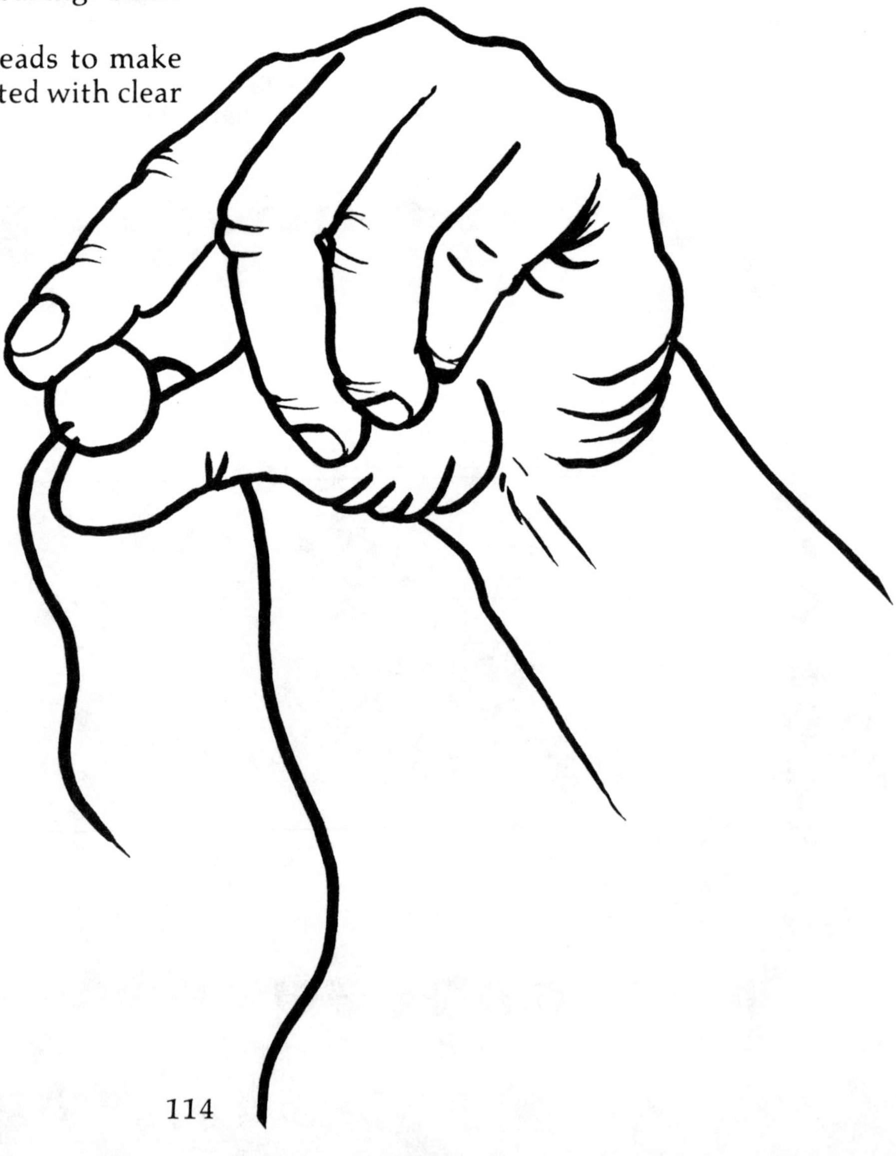

MACRAME ROSARY   Grades 5-8

Materials Needed:

String (heavier quality)
Scissors
Wooden cross (approx. 2") with hole in top for string to slide through
Diagram of rosary

The length of string needed per student will depend upon the thickness of the string and the skill of the students to make knots close together. Three to five feet of 20 ply string is needed for each rosary. Make a sample of a rosary to test for length needed and tightness of knots.

Procedure:

1. Make ten single knots evenly spaced in a piece of string for the *Hail Marys.*
2. Make a double or triple knot for the *Our Fathers.*
3. Continue around for all five decades. Use a workable length (approximately 18") to knot one decade. Do five lengths or decades and double or triple knot them together. This knot becomes the *Our Father* knot.
4. Attach a piece of string (approximately 12") to the cross. Make a double or triple knot, space, three single knots, space, one double or triple knot.
5. Attach this piece to the large part of the rosary in the proper place. (See diagram.)
6. Trim excess string.

You may want to make arrangements to have these rosaries blessed.

BEATITUDES PLAQUE   Grades 1-4

Materials Needed:

Drawing paper (9" x 12" or 12" x 16")
Colored construction paper
Crayons, colored chalk or tempera paint
Copies of the Beatitudes
Glue or stapler
Paint shirts and brushes if paint is used
Old magazines
Scissors

Before Class:

Prepare multiple strips of paper with one Beatitude printed on each strip.

Procedure:

1. Draw a picture of Jesus sitting on top of a hill. Draw some of his disciples.
2. Cut out magazine pictures of people sharing and helping others. Glue these pictures on the picture of Jesus you made.
3. Glue or staple one or more of the Beatitude strips of paper to your picture.
4. Title your picture if desired.
5. Glue or staple your picture on a piece of colored construction paper to make a frame.

BEATITUDES BANNER   Grades 5-8

Materials Needed:

Material for banners: old white sheets, unbleached muslin or runners from church weddings
Pencils
Felt tip pens
Dowel rods
Yarn
Stapler or needle and thread

Before Class:

Make copies of suggested symbols. Write the word *Beatitudes* on the blackboard before class.

Procedure:

Help the students understand that they can BE-a-good-ATTITUDE in the world by following Jesus in his mission of reaching out to others.

1. Direct the students to design a simple picture or symbol to represent their chosen Beatitude. Use the suggested symbol sheet to help the students with ideas.
2. Write the words of the Beatitude on the banner and draw a picture or symbol to demonstrate the Beatitude.
3. Color with felt tip pens, using bright, happy colors. Outline the symbol in black. (optional)
4. Fold the top of the banner down and staple or sew to make a pocket for a dowel rod.
5. Slip the dowel rod through the pocket and tie yarn to each end of the dowel rod.

117

PINE CONE SHEPHERD   Grades 1-4

Jesus taught the two greatest commandments of how we are to love God with all our hearts and to love our neighbors as ourselves. Loving our neighbors and ourselves is a way of loving God. These little pine cone shepherds will carry the sign "Love One Another" to remind us how to love.

Materials Needed:

Large pine cone — 1 per student
2½" styrofoam ball — 1 per student
Glue
Pipe cleaners
Sequins and pins
Felt or material (solid colors)
"Love One Another" printed on small strips of paper
Optional: Cardboard for stand

Before Class:

Make up a sufficient supply of "Love One Another" signs.

Procedure:

1. Glue the styrofoam ball to the top of the pine cone.
2. Glue or pin two sequins for the eyes and one for the nose (or use felt).
3. Wrap a pipe cleaner around the pine cone for arms.
4. Glue a piece of felt or material for the head piece covering.
5. Glue the small "Love One Another" sign between hands.
6. Optional: The pine cone may be glued to a small piece of cardboard to use as a stand.

PINE CONE SHEPHERD   Grades 5-8

Materials Needed:

Large pine cone — 1 per student
2½" styrofoam ball — 1 per student
Old nylon stockings
Cotton balls
Brown or tan thread
Sequins and pins
Scrap material (solid colors) or felt material
Thin gold or silver braid or twine
Pipe cleaners or chenille stems
Pen
White paper
Scissors
White glue or "Sobo" glue
Optional: #32 tie wire

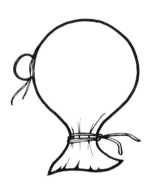

Procedure:

1. If necessary, carve a small hole in bottom of styrofoam ball to have it "sit" properly on pine cone (or break off a few petals of pine cone to make it flat on top). Do not attach styrofoam ball yet.
2. To make "head" and "nose," work with a partner:
   (a) Cover entire styrofoam ball with a piece of old nylon. Make sure there is enough material to gather for neck.
   (b) Add a tiny piece of cotton underneath the nylon to make the nose. Have your partner hold the "head," keeping the nylon tight around the neck while you "pinch" the nose in shape. Tie a piece of thread around the nose to hold the shape.
   (c) Keeping the nylon tight around the neck, tie another piece of thread around the neck.
3. Glue the head to the top of the pine cone. Wrap more thread around the neck and pine cone to anchor securely. (Optional: Attach the head to the cone with #32 tie wire. Wrap wire tightly around ball and cone.)
4. To make features.
   (a) Eyes — Use two sequins and pins.
   (b) Beard — Fluff out a piece of cotton and glue to chin area.
   (c) Arms — Wrap a pipe cleaner around the pine cone body.
5. Cut and glue material to form headpiece for the shepherd.
6. Tie a piece of gold or silver braid around the forehead.
7. Print "Love One Another" on a small piece of white paper and glue it to the hands of the shepherd.

THIS IS YOUR LIFE: Something Special for a Special Friend   Grades 1-8

Materials Needed:

Magazines with colored pictures
Scissors
Glue
Assorted decorations (colored paper, doilies, lace, stickers, etc.)
Sheet of heavy white cardboard

Procedure:

1. Look through magazines. Cut out anything that reminds you of the person for whom you are making this gift. If the person loves music, look for pictures with a music format. For sports, use basketball, soccer, skating, etc. Consider favorite foods and hobbies. Use pictures, words, or a short story or poem about your friend.
2. Arrange the items attractively before you glue them down on the sheet of white cardboard. Decorate with lace, colored stars, etc. Try to remember how special your friend is and say it in pictures.

LIVING STONES   Grades 1-8

St. Peter wrote about Jesus in the Bible as the "living stone" who was rejected by the people in power but approved and precious in God's eyes. We, too, are "living stones" (I Peter 2:4 and 5). We are God's building stones of the Church, with Jesus as the cornerstone. God wants to build Church with you and me. Let the stones with our names on them remind us of all the saints who have lived before us. We, too, should strive to become good and loving persons.

If possible, obtain a copy of *Lives of the Saints* or some other book on saints. Have the students read about the saint after whom they were named. Children are delighted to find out about their patron saint. This will help make the rock project more meaningful for the students. You may wish to put the scripture verse I Peter 2:4-5 on the blackboard.

Materials Needed:

Stones (paperweight size), smooth and clean, any shape — 1 per student
Poster, gouache or acrylic paints
Brushes
Paint shirts
Newspapers
Optional: Felt and glue

Before Class:

Wash stones and let them dry so there is a clean surface on which to paint. Make sure the stone has at least one smooth surface.

Procedure:

1. Have the students study their rocks and find the best place to paint their names.
2. Let the students' creativity and imagination flow as they paint and decorate their personal "name stone."
3. Optional: Glue felt to the bottom of the stone.
4. Let the students look up their patron saint and read about him or her while the rocks are drying. Grades 1 and 2: While they are painting, tell the students personally about their patron saints.

PUPPETS   Grades 1-8

Briefly discuss with the students what the world would be like without laws and rules for protection of person and property. Divide the class into two groups. Have one group list as many rules as they can think of. Have the other group think about what kind of rules they would have if they could make them. Using their puppets, let the groups present a puppet show, demonstrating what could happen to them without good and protective rules. For example, what would happen if we didn't have rules for bedtime? What if we didn't have rules on when to go to school? What if we didn't have rules for crossing the street? Using their ideas, have the students present a skit with the puppets to show how rules are a part of their life.

STICK PUPPETS   Grades 1-4

Materials Needed:

Catalogs
Greeting cards
Magazines
Scissors
Glue or paste
Cardboard
Popsicle sticks

Procedure:

1. Cut pictures out of old cards, catalogs, magazines, etc.
2. Paste the picture on cardboard. Trim the cardboard to be the shape of the picture outline. Make a long handle out of the cardboard or use a popsicle stick. Leave other parts of the picture for scenery around your picture. For example, leave a tree in the background in a picture where a boy is throwing a ball, etc.

BOX PUPPETS   Grades 1-4

Materials Needed:

Small boxes such as cereal boxes — 1 per student
Construction paper
Scissors
Glue
Fabric scraps
Yarn

Before Class:

Score the box in the middle of the front side and cut down both sides. Leave the back all in one piece. Fold the box in half.

Procedure:

1. Cover the box with construction paper.
2. Create a face on the box using construction paper, fabric scraps, yarn, etc.
3. Put your thumb in the bottom of the box and your fingers in the top to make the puppet move.

SOCK PUPPETS   Grades 1-8

Materials Needed:

Ice cream, oatmeal or other round containers — 1 per student
Odds and ends of rickrack, yarn, cotton, felt, fabric, etc.
Buttons
Sock — 1 per student
Glue or needle and thread
Scissors

Procedure:

Push container into toe of sock to create a nose. Glue or sew on the mouth, eyes, etc.
Add hair and ears.

PAPER BAG PUPPETS   Grades 1-8

Materials Needed:

Paper bag (small lunch bag size) — 1 per student
Odds and ends of rickrack, yarn, cotton, felt, fabric, etc.
Buttons
Paint, crayons or magic markers
Glue
Scissors

Procedure:

Draw a face on the bottom flap of the paper bag or glue on odds and ends to make a face on the flap. Add yarn or fabric for hair, cap, ears, etc. on your puppet.

LET YOUR LIGHT SHINE PAPER CANDLES   Grades 1-4

Materials Needed:

Cardboard tubes (toilet paper rolls, paper towel rolls, etc.) — 1 per student
Tissue paper in red, yellow, orange colors
Aluminum foil
Glue or tape
Scripture verses (e.g., "You are the light of the world," Matt. 5:14, "Let your Light Shine," Matt. 5:15)
Optional: Cardboard or posterboard

Before Class:

Prepare scripture verses on the symbolism of light.

Procedure:

1. Cover the tube with aluminum foil and tape or glue in place.
2. Insert tissue paper in the top of the tube to resemble a flame. Glue or tape into place if necessary.
3. Glue or tape a scripture verse to the candle.
4. Optional: Glue or tape the candle to a round piece of cardboard or posterboard to make a base for the candle to stand. The cardboard should be cut 2" to 3" larger than the tube.

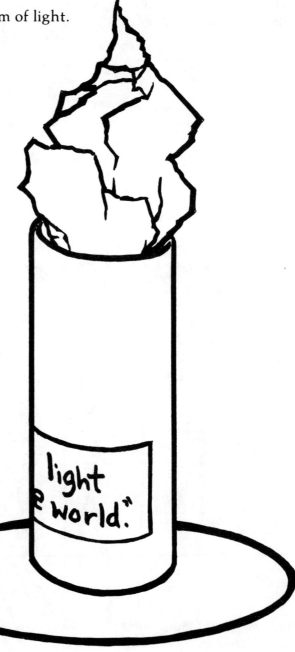

LET YOUR LIGHT SHINE SAND CREATION CANDLES   Grades 5-8

Materials Needed:

Colored "sand" (see recipe below)
Spoons
Small baby food jars — 1 per student
5# salt
Electric frying pan
1 lb. coffee cans
Containers for the "sand"
Powdered tempera paint
Toothpicks
Parafin wax
Wicks (2" to 3" long) — 1 per student

Colored "Sand" Recipe:

Ingredients: salt and powdered tempera paint. Buy 5 lbs. of salt. Fill a small container ½ full of salt. Add a few tablespoons of powdered tempera paint and mix. Add more powdered tempera paint until desired color is reached. Fill one container with each of the following colors: blue, brown, yellow, orange, red or any suitable "desert" colors. (You could use real sand if you prefer.)

Before Class:

Mix up a sufficient amount of colored "sand."

Procedure:

1. Layer different colors of sand gently into baby food jars. Leave room at the top for wax (approximately 1").
2. Gently poke a toothpick down into the sand between the glass and the layers of sand to make designs.
3. Carefully place a wick in the center of the sand.
4. Gently spoon layers of wax on the top. Hold the wick in place until the wax hardens.

To Melt Wax: Have an adult assistant assigned to this task. Partially fill an electric frying pan with water. Place squares of parafin wax in a small 1 lb. coffee can and set in the frying pan. Heat water just enough to melt wax. Bend an old tablespoon to spoon out wax to cover the "sand" creations. The wax seals the sand from moving or spilling and creates a candle.

We Are A Sign To Others

MONOGRAMS   Grades 5-8

Materials Needed:

Paper
Cloth
Felt
Pipe cleaners
Lace
Corkwood
Scissors or razor blades
Needle and thread or glue
Paper
Pencils

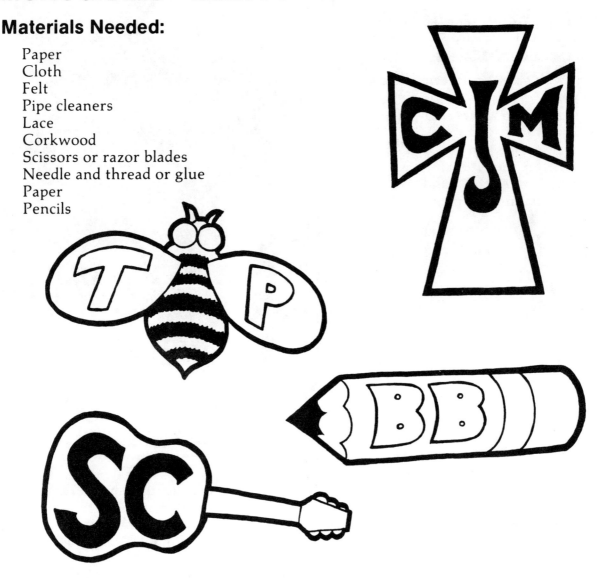

Procedure:

Monograms can be used on clothing, luggage or shoes, etc. Shapes, kinds of letters and size can vary greatly for monograms. Some suggestions are illustrated. Some monograms are easier to cut with a razor blade than with a scissors. Monograms must be designed to fit into a specific size or shape. Students create their monogram's own size and shape. Monograms shaped from pipe cleaners are tacked into place with a needle and thread. They must be removed before laundering or they will rust. Other monograms are sewed or glued, depending on materials used.

Have the students think about what they have learned this year. Have them design their own monogram to symbolize one particular idea. Some ideas are saints, friendship, gifts and talents, prayer, etc.

This can be a two-session project. The first session would give students time to get their thoughts down on paper in the form of a realistic monogram. The second session would be for the students to actually create their own monogram.

Our Responsibility As Church

SHOEBOX SCENE   Grades 3-8

Discuss with the students how the Church is the spiritual guide to the world. Using this theme, have the students create a shoebox scene. They could depict what the Christian's responsibility is to other people: family members, minorities, refugees, immigrants, the poor, the Church, the local community and the world.

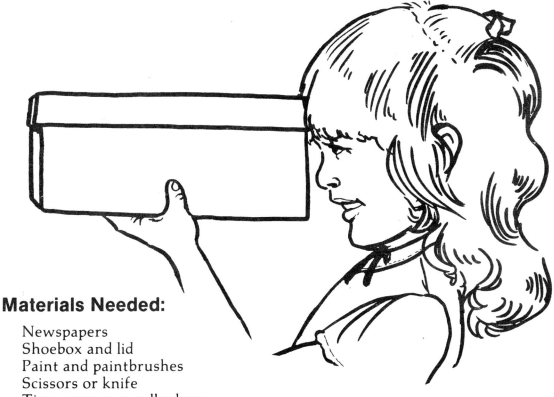

Materials Needed:

Newspapers
Shoebox and lid
Paint and paintbrushes
Scissors or knife
Tissue paper or cellophane
Odds and ends for scene (i.e., twigs, aluminum foil, matches, sponge, thread, etc.)

You may want to have aides for the younger students.

Procedure:

1. Cut a small hole in one end of the box with a scissors or a knife. Cut a round or oblong hole in the lid at one end.
2. With the lid off, paint a scene on the bottom of the box. Keep checking back through the hole in the end of the box to see what the scene looks like.
3. Put the lid on to see whether the hole is letting in enough light. The hole in the lid needs to be at the end opposite the peep hole.

Request the students to bring their own boxes and other items for their scene. Prepare a list in advance and send it home to the parents.

Various things can be used for the scene. Use crumpled paper for a rough sea, a ship with matches for masts, a matchbox house with a piece of mirror for a lake or aluminum foil for water. Bits of sponge on a twig can be a tree.

The light in the box will change depending upon if you use tissue paper or cellophane over the hole in the lid. Cellophane is best if you have it. Using thread, things such as birds or airplanes can be hung down from the lid.

CRAYON BATIK   Grades 1-8

Think of what you might draw to illustrate trust in God. Pass out scratch paper and pencils for students to draw their idea. Write some ideas from the group on the blackboard. You might suggest a simple drawing of one of the Patriarchs, Abraham and Sarah or Joseph. A picture of a Bible could remind students to trust in God's Word. Another suggestion may be to draw a rainbow. The rainbow is a symbol of God's covenant with the people and is associated with the early patriarch, Noah, in the Book of Genesis.

Materials Needed:

Unbleached muslin or old white sheets
Scratch paper
Pencils
Wax crayons
Dowel rods
Yarn or string
Newspapers
Iron
Stapler or needle and thread
Optional: Felt tip marking pens

You will need aides for this project for the younger students. Also, for all grade levels, you will need an aide in charge of the "ironing."

Before Class:

Cut material into 8" x 12" rectangles or suitable banner size. Cut dowel rods into 10" length or 2" wider than banner.

Procedure:

1. Fold down the top of the material approximately 2". This will be the pocket for the dowel rod.
2. Have the students draw their design in pencil. Keep it simple! One suggestion is to draw and color a rainbow. Students could print "Trust in God" somewhere on their banner. Some students might want to design the words only and color in the letters or use the rainbow as a background for the lettering.
3. Color in the design with wax crayons. Press hard.
4. Place the material upside down between newspaper.
5. Press with a hot iron until crayon wax is gone (about 1 minute). Remove the banner carefully. Change the bottom newspaper to be ready for the next banner.
6. Staple, glue or sew banner around a dowel rod.
7. Tie yarn or string to the ends of the dowel rod to hang the banner.
8. Optional: Students may outline the design with a felt tip marking pen.

Covenant

RAINBOW PICTURE   Grades 1-4

Materials Needed:

Blue finger paint
White paper about 12" x 18"
Sponge
Water
Newspapers
Construction paper — various colors
Rainbow stripe pattern
Glue
Scissors

Procedure:

1. Cover table with newspapers. Put a white sheet of paper on the table and dampen the sheet with a sponge and water. Put about a tablespoon of finger paint on the paper and cover the entire paper with the paint. Make swirling motions.
2. While the paint is drying, wash the students' hands. Have the students make rainbows from construction paper, using various colors for the stripes of the rainbow.
3. Cut out the rainbow stripes.
4. Glue the rainbow stripes to the finger-painted background when it is dry.

Finger Paint Recipe:

Mix 3 Tbs. of sugar with ½ tsp. cornstarch. Add 2 c. cold water and cook over low flame. Stir constantly. Divide mixture into four or five portions and add different food coloring or poster paint to each portion.

Covenant

RAINBOW PICTURE   Grades 1-4

Materials Needed:

Newspapers
Paint and brushes or crayons
White paper or newsprint
Materials for cleaning up

Procedure:

Pass out paper to each student. Remind the students that the rainbow is a symbol of a covenant and God's presence with the people. Have the students draw their own rainbow picture using paints or crayons.

Covenant

SCROLL   Grades 1-8

Materials Needed:

White shelf paper
Black crayons
Two dowel rods 4" longer than the width of the shelf paper
Glue
Ribbon

You will need teacher aides for the younger students.

Procedure:

1. Have the students think about a promise or "covenant" they would make with a friend.
2. Have the students print their promise on the center of the shelf paper. (Grades 1 and 2 will need help with the printing.)
3. Glue a dowel rod to each end of the paper.
4. Glue ribbon to the ends and tie scroll.
5. Have the students share their "covenant" with their friend.

Joseph

STAINED GLASS MOBILES   Grades 3-8

Materials Needed:

Cardboard
Acetate
Aluminum foil
Scissors
India ink
Pencils
Newspapers
Glass stain paint
Cord
Dowel rods, heavy wire or clothes hangers
Mobile patterns

Before Class:

Make ample patterns for the students to use.

Procedure:

1. Cover the tables with newspapers. By tracing on the cardboard, create pieces for the mobile using patterns provided (harp, crown, trumpet, Joseph's coat, shepherd's crook and tablets). Older students can be invited to make their mobile pieces more elaborate by cutting out the center for colored acetate inlays and by decorating the pieces as they desire.
2. Use foil, acetate, india ink, patterns and stained glass paint to make the mobile pieces.
3. Attach cords to each piece and attach to a dowel rod, wire or clothes hanger. Try various lengths until you have the right balance for each element on the mobile.

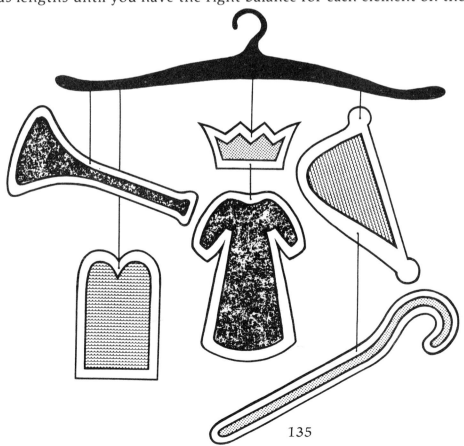

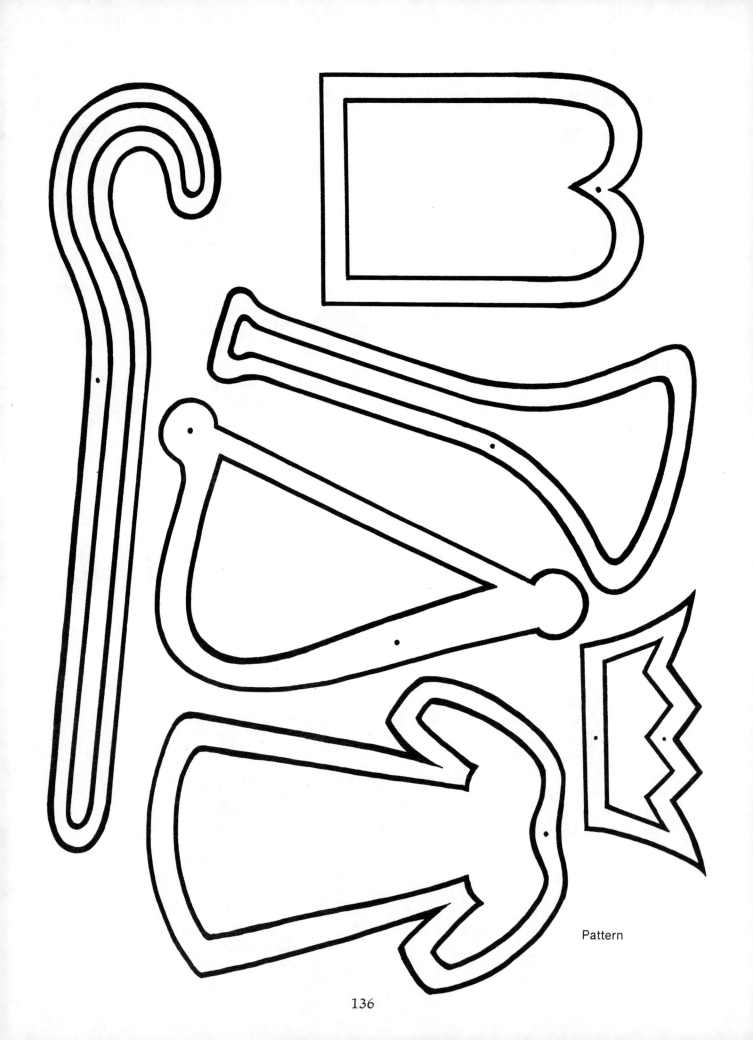

Pattern

136

Moses

SANDPAPER DESERT PAINTING   Grades 1-4

This "sand painting" project will remind us of how Moses led the Israelites through the desert in search of the promised land of freedom and abundance. This journey of the Israelites roots the Christian experience for us today as we view our life as a journey towards God and God's promises.

Materials Needed:

Crayons
Sandpaper, large enough to draw on, 1 piece per student
Optional: Iron and drawing paper

Procedure:

1. Ask the students if they have ever been to a desert. What was it like? Try to get the students to "feel" and create the "mood" of a desert scene: hot, dry, thirsty. To create the mood of "hot" or "dry," have the students use a lot of "warm" or "hot" colors such as orange, red, and yellow in their painting.
2. Have the students draw their desert picture directly on the sandpaper.
3. Press crayons hard in some areas, light in others. The students will have a bright, rough-textured drawing.
4. Optional: To make a print of their drawing, have the students place the drawing, crayon-side down, on a piece of drawing paper. Iron the back side of the sandpaper with a hot iron. Pull the sandpaper and drawing paper apart. Now you have two drawings!

BURNING BUSH BANNER   Grades 1-8

The burning bush is a symbol of the call of Moses to deliver the Israelites from the bondage of the Egyptians. God calls us to show our love by helping and caring for others.

Materials Needed:

8" x 10" burlap piece — 1 per student
Felt pieces of brown, gold, oranges, yellows, reds
Glue
Dowel rod
Yarn
Pencils
Scissors
Patterns

Before Class:

Cut out the burning bush pieces for grades 1-3 so the students only have to arrange the colored "burning bush" pieces on the burlap and glue.

Procedure:

1. Pass out patterns of the various pieces and let the students trace the patterns onto the colored felt.
2. Cut the felt pieces and arrange them on the burlap so that they form a burning bush. Glue the burning bush to the burlap.
3. Fringe the edges of the burlap by pulling out 4-5 rows around the banner.
4. If used for a wall picture, glue a dowel rod on top of the burlap. Tie yarn to the ends of the dowel rod and hang.

Pattern

DESERT "SAND" PAINTING   Grades 5-8

Materials Needed:

Cardboard or wood (about 8" x 10") — one per student
Pencils
White glue
Colored "sand" (recipe below)
Pie tins (paper plates or plastic meat trays may also be used)
Plastic spoons
Newspaper
Optional: Acrylic spray fixative

You will need aides to help with this project.

Colored "Sand" Recipe:

Ingredients: salt and powdered tempera paint. Buy 5# of salt. Fill small coffee can ½ full of salt. Add a few tablespoons of powdered tempera paint and mix. Add more powdered tempera paint until desired color is reached. Fill coffee cans with each of the following colors: blue, brown, yellow, orange and red (or any suitable "desert" colors). You also could use real sand.

Before Class:

Mix up a sufficient amount of colored "sand."

Procedure:

1. Cover the table and floor with newspapers.
2. Spoon a small amount of each color of sand into the pie tins.
3. Draw a few lines with pencil across the cardboard to define sky, mountains, sand, etc. Do not draw in detail.
4. Starting at the top, squeeze glue along sky area. Spread glue thinly over area with fingers.
5. Sprinkle desired color of sand over the sky area. (Skies do not all have to be blue. There are orange and red sunsets.) Let dry a minute. Gently shake off excess sand back into the pie tin.
6. Do the next area in the same manner until the sand painting is completed.
7. Dry flat.
8. Optional: Painting can be sprayed with acrylic spray fixative in two to three coats to make it more permanent. This is especially important if the painting is done on wood.

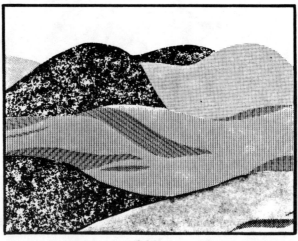

Exodus

TAU CROSS   Grades 1-2

The Tau Cross was the sign made by the Israelites on their doorposts at the Exodus to escape the wrath of the Pharaoh. It was a sign of blessing.

Materials Needed:

Construction paper — black or dark color
White glue
Scissors

Before Class:

On white paper, draw the Tau Cross for each student.

Procedure:

1. Help the students cut out the Tau Cross you have copied.
2. Glue the white Tau Cross to the darker piece of construction paper.
3. Pray the prayer, *Glory to the Father*, together and talk about the blessings God has given each one.

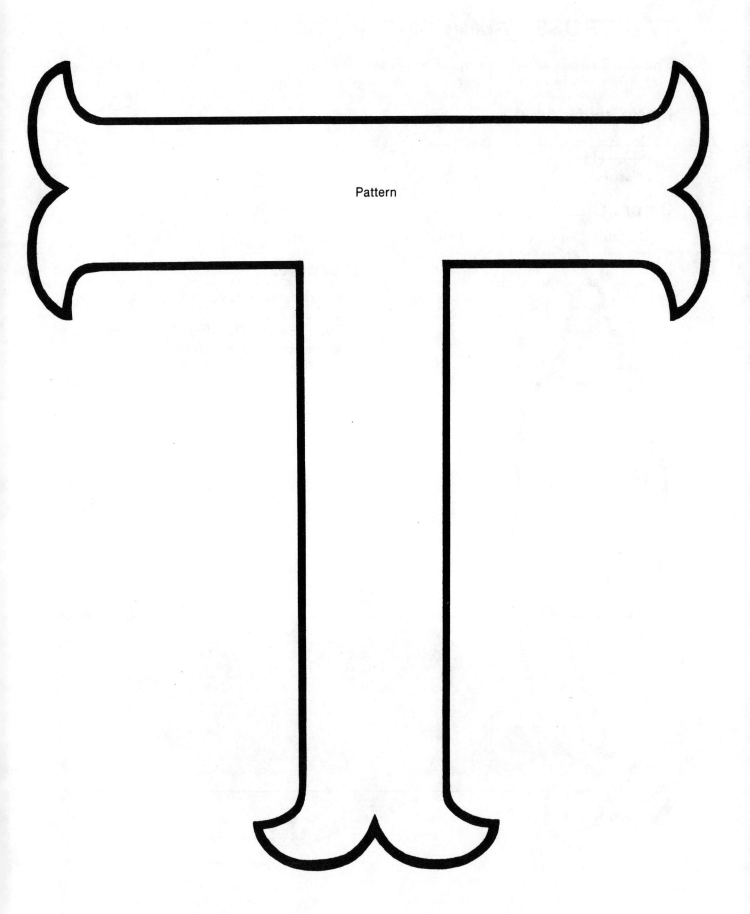

Pattern

TEN COMMANDMENTS CLAY TABLETS   Grades 1-4

Materials Needed:

Newspapers or other table covering
Clay or playdough (see recipe)
Pencil

Recipe for Clay:
1 cup salt
2 cups flour
1 cup water

Mix salt and flour. Add water gradually and mix with hands. Form in balls and seal in a tightly covered container.

Procedure:

1. Soften clay or playdough.
2. Divide in half.
3. Make a tablet as shown in the picture. Flatten the dough and push it into shape.
4. Use a pencil on the clay tablets. Write the Roman numerals to represent the Ten Commandments.
5. Place the tablets on a shelf to dry for 24 hours before the students take the tablets home.

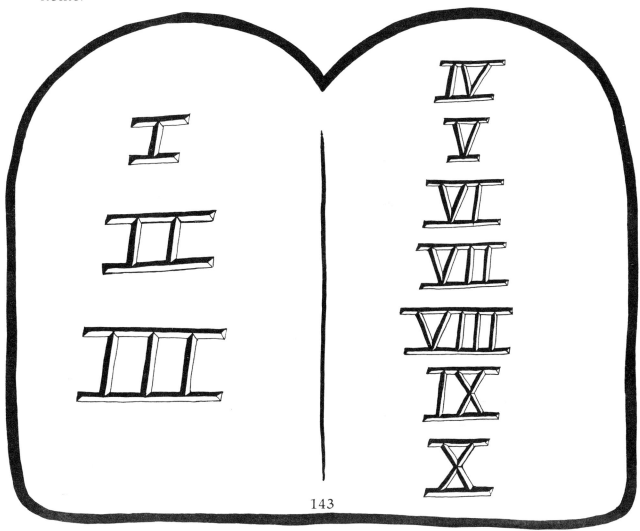

143

God

EYE OF GOD MEXICAN YARN ORNAMENT
(Ojo de Dios) Grades 3-8

The Ojo de Dios, literally translated from the Spanish, means "eye of god" and was a symbol used by the Indians of northwestern Mexico. It has been found as far south as Peru and as far east as Egypt.

Although the Indians did not know God as Jesus, they did know there was a "Great Spirit" greater than themselves. They felt a need for prayer and used this symbol as a request for health and protection.

We can use this as a Christian symbol today by observing that the center is a cross and reflecting on the power of the cross and Jesus' resurrection as a sign of God's love for all. The four beams of the cross reach to the four ends of the earth: north, south, east and west.

Materials Needed:

Two 12" dowel rods or sticks about ¼" thick (twigs, popsicle sticks, toothpicks)
Various balls of yarn in four colors (length depends upon how large you wish the god's-eye to be)
Scissors
One 6" piece of cardboard per student
Optional: Glue

You will need aides to help the younger students.

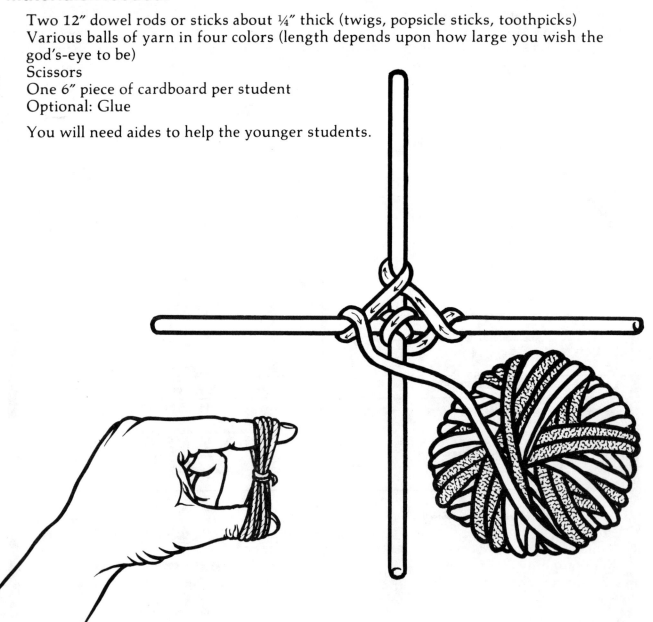

144

Procedure:

1. Glue the sticks together or wrap the yarn around both sticks at right angles with centers matching to secure them in the shape of a cross.
2. Tie the end of one color of yarn around the sticks at their centers so that the knot is in the back. Always work with the front side facing you.
3. Hold the crossed sticks in one hand and the yarn in the other. Turning the cross frame, weave the yarn in a circular manner, wrapping it completely around each stick as you come to it.
4. You may change colors at any time. Tuck the old and new yarn ends under and continue wrapping the new color.
5. Continue wrapping yarn to within three-fourths inch of the stick ends.
6. Trim off excess yarn and knot or tuck yarn end under.
7. Add pompoms to the ends of the sticks if desired. To make pompoms, loop yarn around your thumb and first finger, tie the loop in the center and then cut through the ends.

JEREMIAH PINCH POTS   Grades 1-8

Jeremiah was once sent by God to watch a potter at his wheel. God then told Jeremiah, "As the clay is in the potter's hands, so you are in mine." (Jeremiah 18:1-6)

Materials Needed:

Old shirts
Clay
Sponge
Water
Oil cloth or plastic
Sharp pencil or round toothpick

Tips About Clay:

1. There are many different kinds of clay. Some are self-hardening, others are water-based which you can bake in a regular oven. Keep clay in plastic containers until ready to use.
2. Knead clay with hands until soft. Then make project.

Procedure:

1. Use a piece of plastic or an oil cloth to protect the work table and to prevent the clay from sticking to the table.
2. Break clay into pieces about the size of a tennis ball and roll until completely smooth.
3. Hold ball of clay loosely in the palm of your hand and begin to push the thumb of the other hand down into the center of the ball.
4. With the thumb on the inside and the fingers on the outside, gently squeeze the clay. Hold the clay slightly sideways and rotate slowly.
5. Work from the bottom of the ball and upwards, squeezing and pinching in a continuous spiraling movement until the walls of the pot are ¼" thick.
6. To work the neck, reverse the position of the thumb and fingers and gently squeeze the rim until it is round and even.
7. Smooth out any cracks. If the pot is too dry, dampen it with water on a sponge.
8. Have the students "carve" their first name or initials on the bottom of the pot. Use a sharp pencil or a round toothpick for this.
9. Let the clay pots sit on a shelf for 24 hours before having the students take them home.

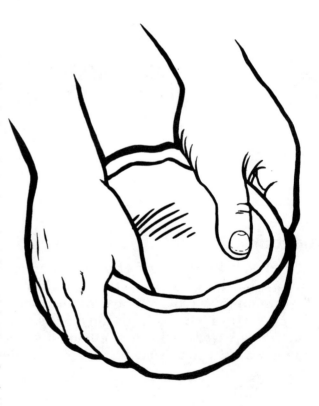

Kings

CROWNS Grades 1-2

Materials Needed:

Construction Paper
Patterns
Glitter
Sequins
Scissors
White glue
Stapler and staples

You will need aides for this project.

Procedure:

1. Cut crowns out of construction paper following the patterns provided.
2. Each student may decorate his or her crown with glitter and sequins.
3. Fit the crown to each student's head. Staple the crown together in the back.

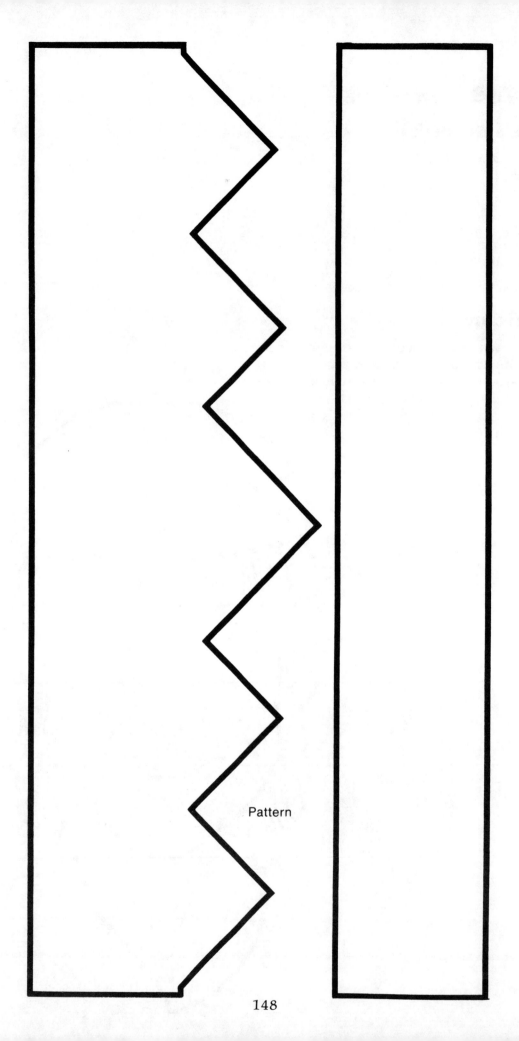

Pattern

148

Kings

SEED PLAQUE Grades 3-8

The symbols of the crown and trumpet suggested here come from an understanding of the prophets' mission. The prophets were spokespersons for God in their own society to recall the leaders and people to God's Word and duty of justice for all. Crowns are symbolic of kingship and trumpets are symbolic of the voice of the prophets.

Materials Needed:

Various kinds of seeds and grains such as: rice, birdseed, flower seeds, orange seeds, grapefruit seeds, etc.
Plywood or pieces of scrap wood
Epoxy glue
Pencils
Popsicle sticks
Pattern
Optional: Food coloring and containers for mixing the rice

Procedure:

1. Optional: You can dye the rice with food coloring in various colors for the crown and trumpet, using a darker shade for the background.
2. Trace the pattern of the crown and trumpet onto a piece of wood.
3. Cover a small space with glue and fill each space with seeds or grains, one at a time. Use various colors. Try not to fill an entire shape with a single color. Use a family of colors which are close in hue, such as green with chartreuse; light, dark, bright and dull shades of blue; red, maroon and pink. Work with popsicle sticks to help keep the various colors in line.

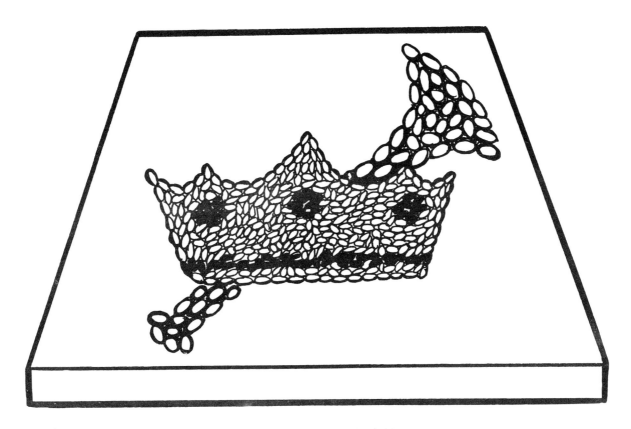

Pattern

CHRISTMAS MURAL   Grades 1-2

Materials Needed:

Plain shelf paper or wrapping paper
Christmas cards
Scissors
Glue
Crayons or magic markers

Procedure:

1. Cut out pictures from Christmas cards.
2. On the strip of shelf paper, glue the pictures to show the sequence of events of Christ's birth.
3. Decorate the mural with crayons or magic markers.
4. Hang the mural on the wall.

Christmas

RIBBON GREETING CARDS Grades 1-8

Materials Needed:

Colored construction paper
Shiny ribbon
Scissors
Glue
Patterns

You may wish to have aides for the younger students.

Procedure:

1. Fold the construction paper in half.
2. Plan a simple design on the front of the card. Fill in the design with strips of ribbon. The strips will vary in length depending upon the design chosen.
3. For a Christmas tree, cut six pieces of green ribbon. Cut the ribbon into three different sizes, each a bit longer than the others. Cut two pieces in each size, shorter for the top and longer for the bottom. Cut a star and tree trunk from gold ribbon. Glue in place. Glue the pieces of green ribbon to the construction paper in the shape of a tree. Open the card and write a greeting.
4. For a holly wreath, cut 25 small triangles from green ribbon and glue to construction paper to form a wreath. Cut 12 circles from red ribbon for the berries. Glue these onto the wreath. Make a bow with gold ribbon and glue it to the bottom of the wreath.
5. For bells, draw two bell shapes from the pattern. On construction paper, glue four strips of ribbon abut ⅛" apart on each bell shape. When the glue is dry, cut out each bell and glue the bells to the Christmas card. Cut two small circles from another piece of ribbon and glue them in place for bell clappers. Fold a length of ribbon and glue it to the tops of the bells.

Note: For grades 1 and 2, use the patterns provided. Have the students glue the ribbons in the areas shown on the patterns to create the tree and/or the bells.

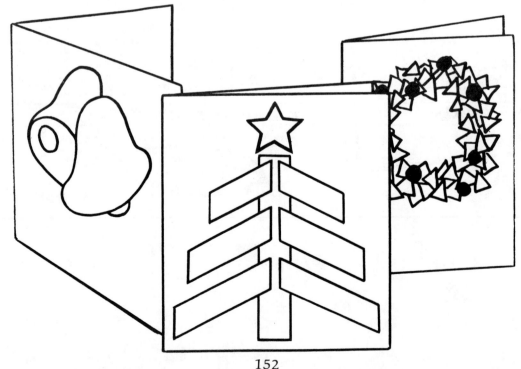

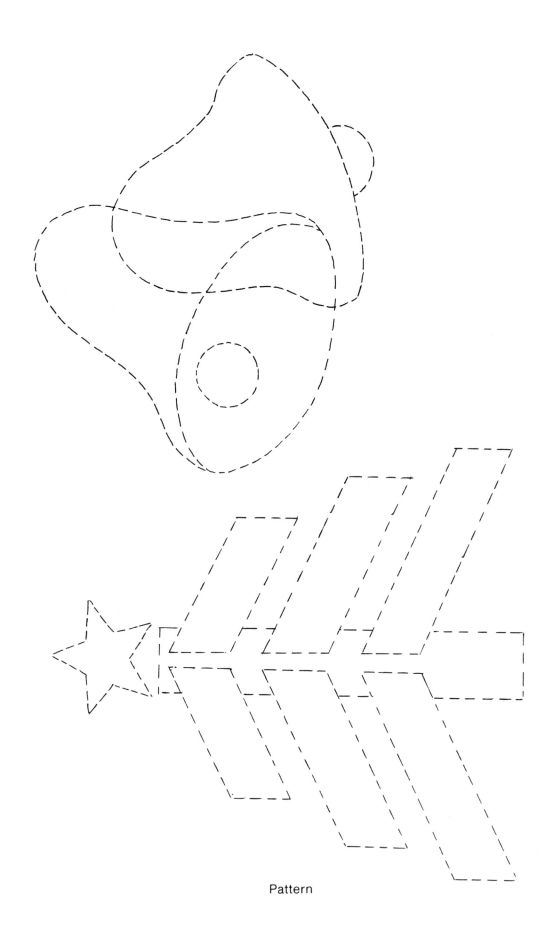

Pattern

CANDLEGLOW   Grades 1-8

Materials Needed:

5½" x 6" deep lilac construction paper — 1 per student
Deep blue, red, silver and gold foil papers
Paste or glue
Scissors
Pencil
Patterns

Before Class:

Have ample pattern pieces cut out. Decide how much of the foil covering you want to have prepared in advance for younger students.

Procedure:

1. Fold the construction paper to measure 5½" x 3". Trace the patterns of the candle and flame from the design onto foil papers and cut them out. Make the candle blue, the inner flame silver, the middle flame red, the outer circle gold.
2. Glue the gold circle to the construction paper equidistant from the top and side edges. Glue the red flame on top, positioning it as in the pattern, putting the silver flame on top of the red flame.
3. Glue the candle into position, overlapping the lower edge of the gold circle.

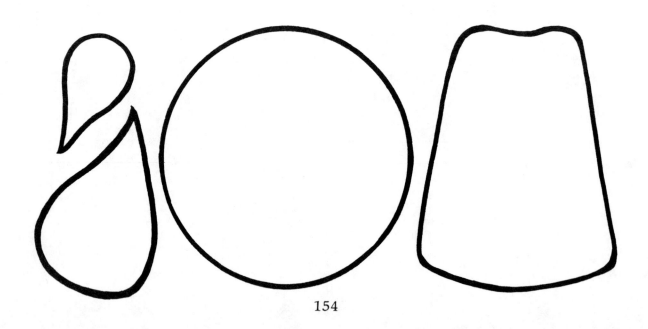

PINE CONE ANGEL   Grades 1-8

Materials Needed:

2½" styrofoam ball — 1 per student
Large pine cone — 1 per student
Foil
Glue
Sequins or glitter
Yarn
Felt
Pipe cleaners
Golf tee — 1 per student

You will need aides for the younger students.

Before Class:

Have pieces cut and ready to glue for grades 1 and 2.

Procedure:

1. Glue styrofoam ball to the top end of the pine cone.
2. Cut wings from foil. Insert and glue wings between the scales of the pine cone.
3. Add features made from sequins, yarn and felt. Form and glue on a pipe cleaner for the arms and halo. Glue on a pipe cleaner to make a stand.
4. Add a golf tee for the trumpet.

Angel Ornament

Assemble an angel as above but add a hanger at the top of the head with fine string or wire. Apply a strip of glue to each wing and add glitter.

CHRISTMAS SYMBOLS   Grades 1-8

This project can be used for all levels, depending upon the complexity of the symbol chosen in the patterns. Grades 1 and 2 may want to use single-piece patterns.

Materials Needed:

Black and white construction paper
Scissors
Glue
Pattern pieces
Pencils

Procedure:

1. Using either candle, angel, bell, Christmas tree or dove pattern, have the students trace around the chosen pattern pieces on either black or white construction paper. If they trace on the black, they would glue the pieces onto a white piece of construction paper. If they trace on white, they would glue the white pieces onto the black construction paper.
2. After each piece of the pattern is cut individually, apply it with glue, designing the angel or whatever pattern is chosen. This will create a positive/negative effect.
3. Older students could be instructed to cut their design into pieces to give a stained glass effect to the finished product.

Pattern

Pattern

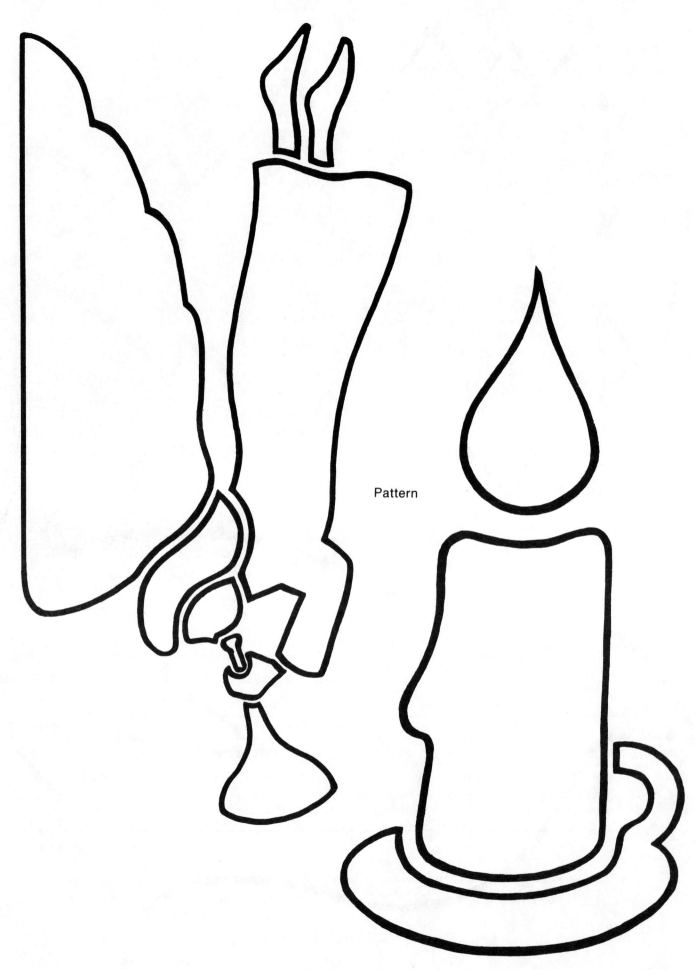

Pattern

Christmas

SILHOUETTES   Grades 3-8

Materials Needed:

Black construction paper
White construction paper
Sharp pencil
Scissors
Assorted colored paper
Cardboard (same size as white paper)
Bright lamp
Ribbon or heavy yarn
Cellophane tape
Glue

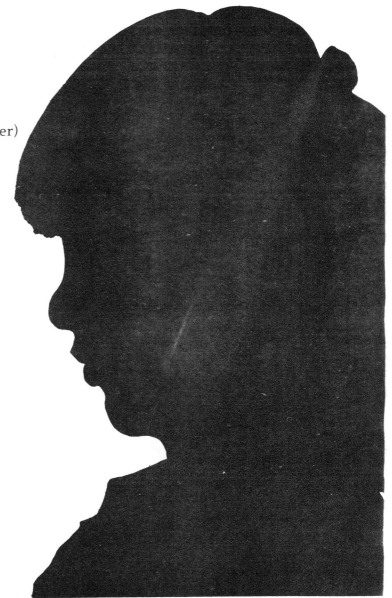

Procedure:

1. Stand or sit between a bright light and an empty wall. Stand sideways so the shadow of your profile falls on the wall. Use the bright lamp to get a strong shadow.
2. Tape a sheet of black construction paper against the wall so your shadow falls on the black paper. The shadow is your silhouette.
3. Ask a friend to trace your silhouette on the paper. Remember to stand or sit still!
4. Carefully cut out the silhouette and set it aside.
5. Glue a sheet of white paper to the cardboard. Place the silhouette in the center and glue it in place.
6. Decorate either with spring flowers, Christmas decorations, hearts, etc., as a border on the white paper. Tape a ribbon or heavy yarn to the back of the silhouette in order to hang it.

This can be a Christmas, Valentine's Day or Mother's Day gift.

CHRISTMAS SHADOW PICTURES   Grades 1-8

Materials Needed:

9" aluminum pie pan
Black felt
Black rickrack or trim
Glue
Scissors
Hanger
Silhouette patterns

You may need aides with this project to either help younger children cut out the silhouettes or to pre-cut the silhouettes.

Procedure:

1. Using a pattern provided, cut the Christmas silhouette and star out of black felt.
2. Glue the scene onto the inside of the pie pan, positioning the star above.
3. Glue rickrack around the edge of the pan for the frame.
4. Glue a hanger on the back of the pie pan.

Pattern

Christmas

CHRISTMAS ANGEL   Grades 5-8

Materials Needed:

Thin cardboard 5″ long and 4″ high for a cylinder 1½″ in diameter (or use an empty toilet tissue roll) — 1 per student
Stapler
Thin cardboard for wings and halo
Brown felt
Braid
Sequins
Beads
Needle and thread
Christmas tree garland
Paste or glue
Scissors
Pinking shears
White and peach felt pieces
1¾″ styrofoam balls — 1 per student
Pattern

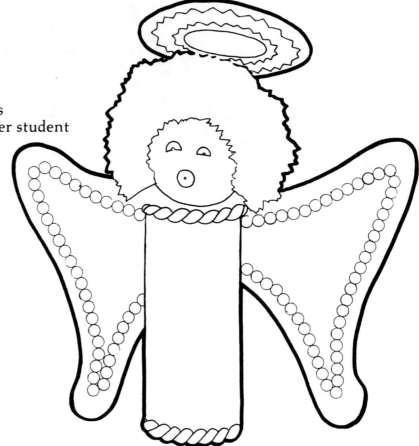

Procedure:

1. Make a cylinder of cardboard 1½″ in diameter. Staple. (Or use the toilet tissue roll.)
2. Wrap felt around the cylinder and sew down the center back. Cover the felt at the top and bottom and add two lengths of braid to trim the bottom and top.
3. Cut a piece of thin cardboard for wings and halo, using the pattern provided. Cut the shape again, using white felt.
4. Cut the inner circle in brown felt for the halo and trim the edges with pinking shears.
5. Cut a smaller wing shape in peach felt and sew to the white felt shape.
6. Paste the inner halo to the white felt and paste the completed wing and halo shape to the cardboard. Decorate the wings with sequins and beads.
7. Paste the wings behind the body cylinder. Cover half of a 1¾″ diameter styrofoam ball with gold material for the head. Add two half sequins for the eyes and a single sequin for the mouth.
8. Paste the head in front of the halo and surround it with about 4½″ of gold Christmas tree garland for hair.

162

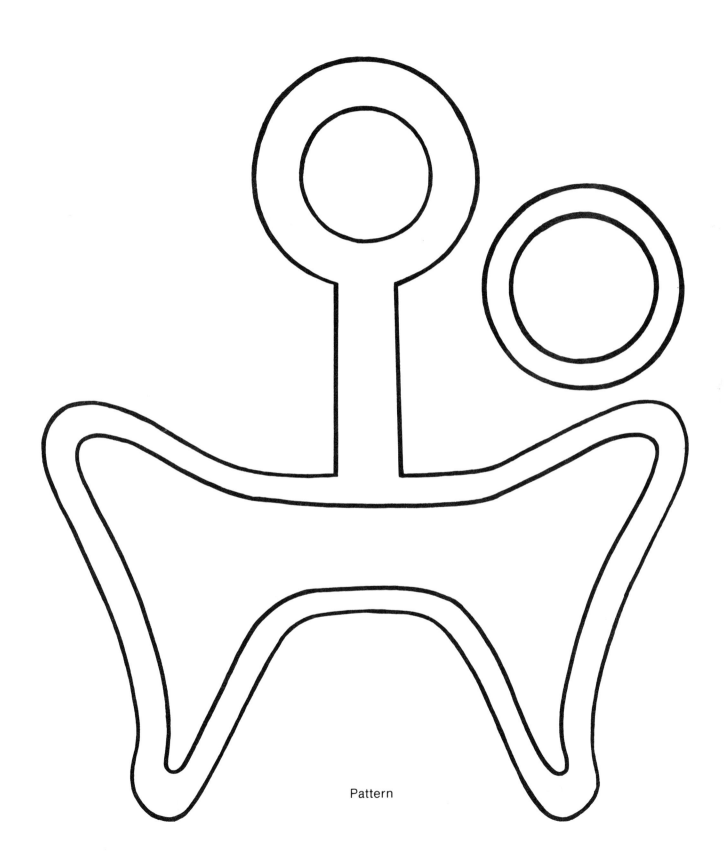

Pattern

CHURCH Program Reference

Cycle A, CHURCH: Our Signs

Cycle A, CHURCH: Our Signs, concentrates on the seven sacraments and the signs and symbols of each sacrament which stand for the deeper spiritual reality behind the visible symbol. Explain to the students that we are able to communicate with others by using symbols. Symbols give information about or stand for something more than they are. For example, a clock is a symbol for time, a barber shop pole for hair cutting, clouds for rain, a heart for love, etc.

One of the earliest symbols used by Christians to represent Jesus Christ is the fish. It was a secret sign for early believers to identify themselves to each other because they were publicly persecuted for their belief in Jesus. The Greek initials for Jesus Christ, "ICHTHUS," spell out the word *fish* and served as a code to other believers. Various crosses, such as the Jerusalem cross and the Chi-Rho, are also ancient symbols which represent Christ. Other symbols represent the seven sacraments.

REVIEW: You might want to use one of the projects from a previous session that you did not already use.

Cycle B, CHURCH: Our Beliefs

Cycle B, CHURCH: Our Beliefs, explores what we as a Church believe and celebrate. The four main beliefs covered here are God, Jesus, Holy Spirit and Resurrection. Students also study the Liturgy of the Church through which these beliefs are celebrated in community.

Three important aspects of faith are: 1) God's revelation to us, 2) our response to God's free gift of faith to us, and 3) how we develop our faith in relationship with God, Jesus and each other. Both the experiential use of symbols and familiar objects from everyday life can be a valuable means of expressing a faith that is difficult to define. These craft projects will help to symbolically represent each belief for the students in an enjoyable way.

Cycle C, CHURCH: Our Story

Cycle C, CHURCH: Our Story, is the story of our religious heritage in the Old Testament which begins some two thousand years before the coming of Jesus into time. This story begins with an introduction of the patriarchs Abraham and Moses and the establishment of the covenant between God and the Hebrew people. The first kings of the Hebrew nation, King Solomon and King David, are introduced. Fidelity to the covenant is the chief concern of the prophets who, in the person of Jeremiah, remind the kings and people to live by their promises and to act justly.

The mission of Jesus completes the hope of the early covenant. The lifestyle of the first Christians reflects a just concern for all in how they shared together in common. The structure of the Church developed out of this experience and the growing need to adjust to an expanding Church.

The crafts outlined in this cycle will reinforce the themes to promote a hands-on experience of learning.

Cycle D, CHURCH: Our Life

Cycle D, CHURCH: Our Life, centers on our responsibility toward each other as members of the Church in the world and some personalities who influence us as models of the Christian lifestyle. The lifestyle of Jesus demonstrates how the Eight Beatitudes and the two greatest commandments to love God and neighbor can lead us to love ourselves in a healthy way and to reach out to others unselfishly.

Mary is presented as the mother of Jesus and mother of the Church. Other saints, such as St. Stephen the first martyr, St. Francis of Assisi who founded the Franciscan Order and St. Elizabeth Ann Seton as the first American saint, are recognized by the process of canonization by the Church to be truly Christian people.

We must remember, however, that there are many other people in every age who love God and have concern for others. Many of the following projects will affirm students in the Christian lifestyle by reinforcing how much they are loved by God.

Topical Index

CREATION/NATURE

EASTER/RESURRECTION

FAITH

FRIENDSHIP

GOD

HOLY SPIRIT

JESUS

LENT

LOVE

Alphabetical Index